Sustainable Cooking

Eco-Friendly Recipes for a Greener Kitchen

Janice Hines

The presentation of the information is without contract or any type of guarantee assurance. The trademarks that are used are without any consent, and the publication of the trademark is without permission or backing by the trademark owner. All trademarks and brands within this book are for clarifying purposes only and are the owned by the owners themselves, not affiliated with this document.

Table of Contents

Chapter 1

Introduction to Sustainable Cooking

What is Sustainable Cooking

Sustainable cooking is an approach to food preparation and consumption that prioritizes environmental, social, and economic sustainability. It involves making mindful choices about what we eat, how we source our ingredients, and how we prepare and consume food. The goal is to reduce our ecological footprint, support local communities, and promote health and well-being.

At its core, sustainable cooking is about making conscious decisions. It begins with understanding the environmental impact of our food choices. The production, transportation, and disposal of food contribute significantly to greenhouse gas emissions, deforestation, water depletion, and pollution. By choosing sustainably sourced ingredients, we can help mitigate these impacts. This means opting for locally grown produce, which reduces the carbon footprint associated with long-distance transportation. It also means choosing organic foods, free from synthetic pesticides and fertilizers that can harm the environment.

Another crucial aspect of sustainable cooking is minimizing food waste. In many parts of the world, a significant portion of food produced is never consumed. This waste not only represents a loss of resources but also contributes to greenhouse gas emissions when it decomposes in landfills. To combat this, we can plan our meals carefully, buy only what we need, and use leftovers creatively. For example, vegetable scraps can be used to make broth, and overripe fruits can be turned into smoothies or baked goods.

Supporting local and seasonal foods is another essential principle. Seasonal produce is often fresher, more nutritious, and less resource-intensive than out-of-season produce that requires energy-intensive greenhouse production or long-distance transportation. By visiting farmers' markets or joining a community-supported agriculture (CSA) program, we can access fresh, seasonal produce while supporting local farmers and reducing our ecological footprint.

Sustainable cooking also involves considering the social and economic aspects of food production. This means supporting fair trade products, which ensure that farmers and workers receive fair wages and work in safe conditions. It also means being mindful of the cultural and social significance of food, respecting traditional practices, and promoting food sovereignty, which allows communities to define their own food systems.

One of the most impactful choices we can make is to incorporate more plant-based foods into our diets. Animal agriculture is a leading cause of deforestation, water pollution, and greenhouse gas emissions. By reducing our consumption of meat and dairy products, we can significantly lower our ecological footprint. Plant-based diets are not only more sustainable but also offer numerous health benefits, including reduced risks of chronic diseases such as heart disease, diabetes, and cancer. Incorporating a variety of fruits, vegetables, legumes, nuts, and grains into our meals can provide all the essential nutrients our bodies need.

In addition to what we eat, how we cook also matters. Energy-efficient cooking methods, such as using pressure cookers, slow cookers, or induction stoves, can reduce energy consumption. Cooking in batches and reheating leftovers can also save energy. It's also important to consider the sustainability of kitchen tools and appliances. Opting for durable, high-quality items that last longer and can be repaired rather than replaced helps reduce waste. When it's time to replace appliances, choosing energy-efficient models can further reduce our environmental impact.

Water conservation is another key element. Cooking often requires significant amounts of water, from washing vegetables to boiling pasta. Simple steps like using a bowl to wash produce instead of running water, reusing pasta water for plants, or steaming vegetables instead of boiling them can help conserve water. Additionally, choosing ingredients that require less water to produce, such as drought-resistant grains and legumes, can make a difference.

Packaging is another area where we can make sustainable choices. Single-use plastics are a major environmental issue, contributing to pollution and harming wildlife. By choosing products with minimal or recyclable packaging, bringing reusable bags and containers when shopping, and storing food in reusable containers, we can reduce our reliance on single-use plastics. Making homemade versions of commonly packaged items, such as bread, yogurt, and snacks, can also cut down on packaging waste.

Sustainable cooking also extends to the way we clean up. Using eco-friendly cleaning products, reducing water waste while washing dishes, and properly disposing of food scraps through composting are all important practices. Composting not only reduces waste but also creates nutrient-rich soil that can be used to grow more food, creating a closed-loop system.

Education and awareness are vital components. Staying informed about the environmental and social impacts of our food choices allows us to make better decisions. This includes understanding food labels, such as organic, fair trade, and non-GMO certifications, and knowing the practices of the brands we support. Sharing knowledge with others and advocating for sustainable food systems in our communities can amplify our impact.

Incorporating these principles into our daily lives might seem daunting at first, but even small changes can make a significant difference. Starting with one or two practices, such as buying local produce or reducing food waste, can gradually lead to a more sustainable lifestyle. Over time, these practices can become second nature, making sustainable cooking an integral part of our routines.

The Importance of Eco-Friendly Recipes

Cooking eco-friendly recipes is more than a culinary trend; it's a vital practice that can help mitigate the environmental challenges we face today. By choosing ingredients and cooking methods that reduce waste, conserve resources, and support sustainable agriculture, we contribute to a healthier planet and a more resilient food system. The importance of eco-friendly recipes extends beyond environmental benefits to encompass health, economic, and social advantages.

One of the most significant reasons for prioritizing eco-friendly recipes is the reduction of our carbon footprint. The food industry is a major contributor to greenhouse gas emissions, with meat and dairy production being particularly impactful. By incorporating more plant-based recipes into our diet, we can significantly reduce these emissions. Plants generally require fewer resources such as water and land, and they produce fewer emissions compared to animal-based foods. For example, a simple switch from beef to lentils in a recipe can save thousands of liters of water and significantly reduce carbon emissions.

Eco-friendly recipes often emphasize the use of local and seasonal ingredients. This not only supports local farmers and economies but also reduces the environmental impact associated with transporting food over long distances. Foods that are in season and grown locally generally require less energy for transportation and storage. They are also fresher and more nutritious, having spent less time in transit. By visiting farmers' markets or joining community-supported agriculture (CSA) programs, we can access a variety of fresh, local produce that enhances the flavor and nutritional value of our meals.

Reducing food waste is another critical aspect of eco-friendly cooking. In many households, a significant portion of purchased food ends up in the trash. This not only wastes the resources used to produce the food but also contributes to methane emissions from landfills. By planning meals carefully, using leftovers creatively, and composting food scraps, we can minimize waste. For instance, vegetable peels and scraps can be saved to make flavorful broths, and leftover grains can be reinvented into salads or stir-fries.

Eco-friendly recipes also often incorporate whole foods and minimally processed ingredients. These foods are typically healthier, as they contain fewer additives, preservatives, and artificial ingredients. Whole grains, legumes, fresh fruits, and vegetables are staples in eco-friendly recipes, providing essential nutrients while being gentle on the environment. Preparing meals from scratch allows us to control the quality and quantity of ingredients, leading to healthier eating habits and reducing our reliance on heavily packaged convenience foods.

Economic benefits are another compelling reason to embrace eco-friendly recipes. Cooking with seasonal, local produce and whole foods can be more cost-effective than relying on processed and out-of-season items. Bulk buying staples like grains, beans, and nuts can further reduce costs and packaging waste.

Additionally, home cooking generally costs less than eating out or buying pre-packaged meals. By making eco-friendly choices, we can save money while supporting sustainable food practices.

Socially, eco-friendly recipes foster a sense of community and connection. Cooking and sharing meals with family and friends can strengthen bonds and create meaningful experiences. Participating in local food initiatives, such as community gardens or cooking classes, can also build a sense of community and shared purpose. These activities not only promote sustainable practices but also encourage knowledge sharing and collaboration.

Moreover, eco-friendly cooking can inspire creativity in the kitchen. Trying new recipes that use a variety of plant-based ingredients, whole foods, and seasonal produce can be a fun and rewarding challenge. It encourages us to experiment with different flavors, textures, and cooking techniques. This creativity can lead to discovering new favorite dishes and a deeper appreciation for the food we eat.

The health benefits of eco-friendly recipes are significant as well. Diets rich in fruits, vegetables, whole grains, and legumes are associated with lower risks of chronic diseases such as heart disease, diabetes, and certain cancers. These foods are high in essential nutrients, fiber, and antioxidants, which support overall health and well-being. By reducing the consumption of processed foods and animal products, we can improve our health while also benefiting the environment.

Eco-friendly recipes also promote food sovereignty, which is the right of people to define their own food systems. By choosing to cook with sustainable ingredients, we support farming practices that are environmentally friendly, socially just, and economically viable. This empowers communities to produce and consume food in ways that align with their values and needs, rather than being dictated by industrial food systems.

Incorporating eco-friendly recipes into our daily lives requires mindfulness and a willingness to change habits. It can start with small steps, such as dedicating one day a week to plant-based meals or committing to buying local produce. Over time, these practices can become second nature, leading to a more sustainable and health-conscious lifestyle. Sharing these practices with others can also amplify our impact, creating a ripple effect that promotes wider adoption of sustainable cooking habits.

Ultimately, the importance of eco-friendly recipes lies in their potential to create positive change. They offer a practical way to address environmental issues, improve health, and support local economies and communities. By making thoughtful choices about what we eat and how we cook, we can contribute to a more sustainable food system. This not only benefits us individually but also helps preserve the planet for future generations.

How to Create a Greener Kitchen

Creating a greener kitchen is an essential step towards living a more sustainable lifestyle. It involves making conscious choices about the materials, appliances, and practices we use in our culinary spaces. By adopting eco-friendly habits, we can significantly reduce our environmental footprint, save money, and create a healthier home environment. The journey towards a greener kitchen starts with understanding the impact of our daily activities and making small, manageable changes that add up over time.

The foundation of a greener kitchen begins with energy-efficient appliances. Older appliances tend to consume more energy, contributing to higher utility bills and greater environmental impact. When it's time to replace an appliance, look for models with the Energy Star label, which signifies that they meet stringent energy efficiency guidelines. Investing in energy-efficient refrigerators, dishwashers, and ovens can lead to significant energy savings. Additionally, using smaller appliances like toaster ovens and microwaves for smaller meals can reduce energy consumption compared to heating up a large oven.

Lighting is another area where we can make eco-friendly improvements. Replacing incandescent bulbs with LED lights can reduce energy usage by up to 80%. LEDs also last longer, reducing the frequency of replacements and the associated waste. Consider installing dimmer switches and motion sensors in areas like the pantry or under-cabinet lighting to further conserve energy. Natural light is the most sustainable option, so maximize the use of windows and skylights to brighten your kitchen during the day.

Water conservation is crucial in a greener kitchen. Simple habits like fixing leaky faucets, installing low-flow aerators, and using dishwashers efficiently can make a big difference. Dishwashers typically use less water than hand-washing, especially when they are fully loaded. If hand-washing is necessary, fill one basin with soapy water and another with rinse water instead of letting the tap run continuously. Also, consider collecting gray water from rinsing vegetables to water plants.

Reducing waste is a cornerstone of eco-friendly living. Start by rethinking your approach to food storage. Invest in reusable containers made of glass or stainless steel instead of relying on single-use plastic bags and wraps. Beeswax wraps are a fantastic alternative for covering bowls and wrapping sandwiches. For shopping, bring reusable grocery bags and produce bags to minimize plastic waste. Buying in bulk and choosing products with minimal packaging can also significantly reduce waste.

Composting is an effective way to handle food scraps and organic waste. A compost bin in your kitchen can collect fruit and vegetable peels, coffee grounds, eggshells, and other compostable materials. Composting not only reduces the amount of waste sent to landfills but also creates nutrient-rich soil for gardening. If you don't have outdoor space for a compost pile, consider a countertop composting unit or look into community composting programs.

Cleaning products are another area where greener choices can be made. Many conventional cleaning products contain harsh chemicals that can harm the environment and our health. Opt for eco-friendly cleaning products that use natural ingredients and are biodegradable. Alternatively, you can make your own cleaning solutions using simple ingredients like vinegar, baking soda, and lemon juice. These homemade cleaners are effective, affordable, and safe for the environment.

Mindful cooking practices also contribute to a greener kitchen. Plan meals ahead to reduce food waste and avoid last-minute trips to the store. Batch cooking and freezing portions can save time and energy. When cooking, use lids on pots to retain heat and cook food faster, and match pot sizes to burner sizes to avoid wasting energy. Cutting food into smaller pieces can also reduce cooking time. Another tip is to turn off the oven or stove a few minutes before the food is fully cooked, allowing residual heat to finish the job.

Sourcing sustainable ingredients is a key aspect of creating a greener kitchen. Choose organic and locally grown produce whenever possible. Organic farming practices reduce the use of harmful pesticides and fertilizers, while local produce requires less transportation, reducing carbon emissions. Supporting farmers' markets and joining a community-supported agriculture (CSA) program can provide access to fresh, seasonal produce while supporting local farmers. Growing your own herbs and vegetables, even in small spaces like windowsills or balconies, can further reduce your environmental impact.

Reducing meat consumption is another powerful way to create a greener kitchen. The production of meat, particularly beef, has a high environmental cost in terms of water usage, land degradation, and greenhouse gas emissions. Incorporating more plant-based meals into your diet can significantly reduce your carbon footprint. Explore vegetarian and vegan recipes that utilize a variety of grains, legumes, nuts, seeds, fruits, and vegetables. Not only are these foods more sustainable, but they also offer numerous health benefits.

Kitchen design and materials also play a role in sustainability. When renovating or designing a kitchen, consider using sustainable materials like bamboo, recycled glass, or reclaimed wood for countertops, cabinets, and flooring. These materials are not only eco-friendly but also add unique aesthetic elements to your kitchen. Choose non-toxic paints and finishes to improve indoor air quality. Additionally, incorporating elements like energy-efficient windows, proper insulation, and ventilation can create a more sustainable and comfortable kitchen environment.

Education and community involvement are essential for sustaining green practices. Stay informed about new sustainable products, technologies, and practices. Share your knowledge and experiences with friends, family, and neighbors to inspire them to adopt greener habits. Participate in local environmental initiatives, such as clean-up drives, tree planting activities, or sustainability workshops. By fostering a community of environmentally conscious individuals, we can amplify our impact and create a larger movement towards sustainability.

Creating a greener kitchen is an ongoing process that evolves with new knowledge and technologies. Start with small, manageable changes and gradually incorporate more sustainable practices into your daily routine. Every step taken towards a greener kitchen contributes to a healthier planet and a more sustainable future. The choices we make in our kitchens have far-reaching effects, influencing not only our immediate environment but also the broader ecosystem.

Benefits of Sustainable Eating

Sustainable eating is more than just a trend; it's a critical approach to food consumption that benefits our health, the environment, and society as a whole. By choosing foods that are produced in ways that protect the environment, support local economies, and promote animal welfare, we can make a significant positive impact on the world around us. Sustainable eating encompasses a wide range of practices, from selecting seasonal and local produce to reducing food waste and incorporating more plant-based meals into our diets. Each of these practices offers unique benefits, creating a holistic approach to a more sustainable lifestyle.

One of the primary benefits of sustainable eating is its positive impact on the environment. The current industrial food system is a major contributor to environmental degradation, including deforestation, water pollution, and greenhouse gas emissions. By choosing sustainably produced foods, we can help reduce these harmful effects. For instance, eating more plant-based foods and less meat can significantly lower our carbon footprint. Livestock farming is responsible for a large portion of methane emissions, a potent greenhouse gas. By opting for plant-based proteins like beans, lentils, and nuts, we can reduce the demand for livestock farming and its associated environmental impacts.

In addition to reducing greenhouse gas emissions, sustainable eating practices can also help conserve water. Agriculture accounts for about 70% of global freshwater use, and much of this is used for irrigation in conventional farming. Sustainable farming practices, such as organic farming and permaculture, often use water more efficiently and help maintain soil health, which can reduce the need for irrigation. By choosing foods grown using these methods, we support the conservation of this vital resource.

Supporting biodiversity is another crucial benefit of sustainable eating. Industrial agriculture often relies on monocultures, where a single crop is grown extensively. This practice can deplete soil nutrients and make crops more vulnerable to pests and diseases, leading to increased use of chemical fertilizers and pesticides. In contrast, sustainable farming practices often involve crop rotation and the cultivation of diverse crops, which can enhance soil health and reduce the need for chemical inputs. By choosing foods from diverse farming systems, we help promote biodiversity and the resilience of our food systems.

Sustainable eating also has significant health benefits. Foods produced using sustainable methods are often fresher and more nutrient-dense than their conventionally produced counterparts. For example, organic fruits and vegetables are typically grown without synthetic pesticides and fertilizers, which can result in higher levels of certain nutrients and antioxidants. Additionally, sustainably raised meat and dairy products are often free from hormones and antibiotics, reducing our exposure to these substances. By eating a diet rich in sustainably produced foods, we can improve our overall health and well-being.

Economic benefits are another important aspect of sustainable eating. By choosing to buy local and seasonal produce, we support local farmers and economies. This not only helps keep money within our communities but also reduces the environmental impact associated with transporting food over long distances. Farmers' markets, community-supported agriculture (CSA) programs, and farm-to-table restaurants are all great ways to access fresh, local produce and support sustainable agriculture. Moreover, reducing food waste can also lead to significant cost savings. Planning meals, buying only what we need, and creatively using leftovers can help reduce the amount of food that ends up in the trash, saving money in the process.

Social benefits are also a key component of sustainable eating. By supporting sustainable food systems, we can help create more equitable and just food systems. Many sustainable farming practices prioritize fair labor practices and the well-being of workers. This means that by choosing sustainably produced foods, we are also supporting better working conditions and fair wages for farmworkers. Additionally, sustainable eating can foster a sense of community and connection. Participating in local food initiatives, such as community gardens or food co-ops, can help build relationships and strengthen community bonds.

Reducing food waste is a critical aspect of sustainable eating. In many parts of the world, a significant portion of food produced is never consumed, which represents a colossal waste of resources. By adopting practices to reduce food waste, such as meal planning, proper food storage, and composting, we can make a substantial difference. Composting food scraps not only reduces the amount of waste sent to landfills but also creates valuable organic matter that can enhance soil health and support sustainable farming practices.

Sustainable eating also involves being mindful of the packaging associated with our food. Single-use plastics and excessive packaging contribute to pollution and waste. By choosing products with minimal or recyclable packaging, bringing reusable bags and containers, and avoiding single-use plastic items, we can reduce our environmental footprint. Many bulk food stores and farmers' markets offer opportunities to buy food with less packaging, making it easier to make sustainable choices.

Educating ourselves and others about sustainable eating is essential for creating lasting change. Understanding the environmental, health, and social impacts of our food choices can empower us to make more informed decisions. Sharing this knowledge with friends, family, and our wider communities can inspire others to adopt sustainable eating practices. Advocacy for policies that support sustainable agriculture and food systems is also crucial. By advocating for change at the local, national, and global levels, we can help create a more sustainable food system for everyone.

Incorporating more plant-based meals into our diet is one of the most effective ways to practice sustainable eating. Plant-based foods generally require fewer resources to produce and have a lower environmental impact compared to animal-based foods. Exploring vegetarian or vegan recipes can introduce us to a variety of delicious and nutritious meals. Even small changes, like participating in Meatless Mondays or choosing plant-based options a few times a week, can make a significant difference.

Sustainable eating also means being conscious of food sourcing. Choosing certified organic, fair-trade, and sustainably sourced products supports practices that are better for the environment and workers. Certifications like Fair Trade, Rainforest Alliance, and Organic provide assurance that the products meet certain environmental and social standards. When available, choosing these certified products can help us make more sustainable food choices.

Ultimately, the benefits of sustainable eating extend beyond individual health and wellness. They encompass broader environmental, economic, and social dimensions, creating a more holistic approach to food consumption. By making mindful choices about what we eat and how our food is produced, we contribute to a more sustainable and just world. Sustainable eating is not about perfection but about making better choices more often. Every small step towards sustainability adds up, creating a collective impact that can drive significant change.

Tips for Reducing Waste

Reducing waste is an essential practice in our quest for a more sustainable and environmentally friendly lifestyle. From the moment we purchase items to how we dispose of them, every step offers an opportunity to minimize waste and its harmful impacts. It may seem daunting at first, but with a few practical tips and a shift in mindset, anyone can make a meaningful difference.

One of the most effective ways to reduce waste is by adopting a minimalist approach to consumption. This means being mindful of what we buy and only purchasing what we truly need. Before making any purchase, consider whether the item is necessary or if there are alternatives that might be more sustainable. For instance, instead of buying new clothes on a whim, look into second-hand stores, clothes swaps with friends, or even learning to mend and upcycle existing garments. By choosing quality over quantity, we can reduce the frequency of purchases and the overall waste generated.

In the kitchen, reducing food waste can save money and significantly lower our environmental footprint. Start by planning meals and creating shopping lists to avoid overbuying. Store food properly to extend its shelf life; for example, keep leafy greens in a container with a damp cloth to prevent wilting. Embrace the art of using leftovers creatively—transforming yesterday's dinner into today's lunch can be both fun and resourceful. Composting food scraps is another excellent way to minimize waste. By turning organic waste into nutrient-rich compost, we can enrich our gardens and reduce the amount of waste sent to landfills.

Single-use plastics are a major contributor to waste, and reducing our reliance on them is crucial. Swap out disposable items for reusable alternatives: carry a reusable water bottle, bring your own shopping bags, and use cloth napkins instead of paper ones. Investing in a set of reusable utensils and a travel mug can also significantly cut down on waste when eating out or grabbing a coffee on the go. Many stores now offer discounts for customers who bring their own containers, providing an added incentive to make the switch.

Packaging waste is another area where we can make substantial improvements. Opt for products with minimal or eco-friendly packaging, and avoid items wrapped in excessive plastic. When possible, buy in bulk to reduce packaging waste. Many grocery stores have bulk sections where you can fill your own containers with grains, nuts, and other dry goods. Additionally, consider supporting local farmers' markets, where produce often comes without packaging and buying directly from the source reduces transportation emissions.

The bathroom is another area ripe for waste reduction. Replace disposable razors with a durable safety razor, and switch to bar soap and shampoo bars to eliminate plastic bottles. Bamboo toothbrushes are a sustainable alternative to plastic ones, and they can be composted after use. For feminine hygiene, consider reusable menstrual products like cloth pads or menstrual cups, which not only reduce waste but can also save money over time.

Electronics and batteries are a significant source of waste, and proper disposal is crucial to prevent harmful chemicals from leaching into the environment. Whenever possible, repair or upgrade electronics instead of discarding them. Many communities offer e-waste recycling programs that safely process old electronics. Rechargeable batteries are a more sustainable option compared to single-use ones, and they can significantly reduce the number of batteries that end up in landfills.

Reducing paper waste is another practical step. Go digital whenever possible—opt for electronic bills, statements, and receipts. Use both sides of paper when printing and reuse scrap paper for notes. Investing in a whiteboard or a reusable notebook can also help cut down on paper usage. At home, consider switching to cloth towels and napkins instead of paper products, which can add up over time.

When it comes to household cleaning, many store-bought products come in single-use plastic containers and contain harmful chemicals. Making your own cleaning solutions using natural ingredients like vinegar, baking soda, and lemon juice can reduce waste and provide a healthier alternative for your home. Reusable cleaning cloths and mop pads can also replace disposable ones, further minimizing waste.

Gift-giving and celebrations often generate a lot of waste, but there are sustainable alternatives. Choose gifts that are meaningful and have a long lifespan, such as experiences, handmade items, or second-hand treasures. For wrapping, use reusable materials like fabric, scarves, or old newspapers. When hosting events, opt for reusable plates, cups, and utensils instead of disposable ones. These small changes can make celebrations more sustainable without compromising on joy.

Educating ourselves and others about waste reduction is vital for fostering a culture of sustainability. Share tips and resources with friends, family, and colleagues. Join or start local initiatives focused on waste reduction, such as community clean-ups or zero-waste workshops. Advocacy at the local level can also drive broader change—support policies that promote recycling, composting, and sustainable practices in your community.

Another key aspect of reducing waste is understanding the lifecycle of products we use. Researching the materials and processes involved in making everyday items can provide insights into their environmental impact. This knowledge can guide more sustainable choices, such as selecting products made from recycled materials or supporting companies with strong environmental commitments.

Incorporating waste reduction into our daily routines takes time and effort, but the benefits are well worth it. By making small, consistent changes, we can significantly reduce the amount of waste we produce and contribute to a healthier planet. Remember that perfection is not the goal; every effort counts, and even minor adjustments can have a positive impact.

One inspiring story comes from Bea Johnson, a pioneer of the zero-waste movement. She and her family managed to fit a year's worth of their waste into a single mason jar. Her approach emphasizes the "5 Rs": Refuse, Reduce, Reuse, Recycle, and Rot. By refusing unnecessary items, reducing what we need, reusing what we have, recycling responsibly, and composting (rot), we can dramatically cut down on waste.

As we navigate our journey towards reducing waste, it's important to celebrate our successes and learn from our challenges. Each step, no matter how small, brings us closer to a more sustainable lifestyle. By adopting these practical tips and encouraging others to do the same, we can make a collective impact that paves the way for a cleaner, greener future.

Chapter 2

Stocking a Sustainable Pantry

Essential Sustainable Ingredients

Sustainable cooking is a journey that begins with understanding the ingredients we use daily. The choices we make in the kitchen can have profound impacts on our health and the environment. Incorporating essential sustainable ingredients into our diets is a powerful way to promote ecological balance, support local economies, and enjoy nutritious meals. By focusing on whole, minimally processed foods and prioritizing local, seasonal, and organic produce, we can create a sustainable and delicious culinary experience.

One of the cornerstones of sustainable cooking is the use of local and seasonal produce. Fruits and vegetables that are in season not only taste better but also require fewer resources to grow and transport. Visiting farmers' markets or joining a community-supported agriculture (CSA) program can connect us with local farmers and provide access to fresh, seasonal produce. For example, tomatoes bought in the summer from a local farmer are likely more flavorful and have a smaller carbon footprint compared to those shipped from afar during winter. Incorporating seasonal ingredients into our recipes not only supports local agriculture but also reduces the environmental impact associated with long-distance transportation.

Organic produce is another critical component of sustainable cooking. Organic farming practices avoid synthetic pesticides and fertilizers, promoting healthier soil and ecosystems. While organic foods can sometimes be more expensive, prioritizing certain items, especially those known to have higher pesticide residues, can make a significant difference. The Environmental Working Group (EWG) publishes an annual list of the "Dirty Dozen" and "Clean Fifteen" to help consumers make informed choices about which produce to buy organic. By focusing on organic options for the most contaminated fruits and vegetables, we can reduce our exposure to harmful chemicals and support farming practices that are better for the planet.

Whole grains are another essential sustainable ingredient. Unlike refined grains, whole grains retain their bran and germ, providing more nutrients and fiber. They also require less processing, which conserves energy and resources. Incorporating a variety of whole grains such as quinoa, brown rice, farro, and barley into our diets can diversify our nutrient intake and reduce our reliance on highly processed foods. Additionally, many whole grains can be purchased in bulk, reducing packaging waste and often saving money.

Legumes, including beans, lentils, and peas, are powerhouse ingredients in sustainable cooking. They are nutrient-dense, versatile, and have a low environmental footprint compared to animal-based proteins. Legumes are excellent sources of plant-based protein, fiber, and essential vitamins and minerals. They can be used in a myriad of dishes, from soups and stews to salads and spreads. Growing legumes also benefits the soil, as they fix nitrogen, reducing the need for synthetic fertilizers. Incorporating more legumes into our diets can help lower our carbon footprint and promote sustainable agriculture.

Nuts and seeds are another group of sustainable ingredients worth highlighting. They are packed with healthy fats, protein, and essential nutrients. Almonds, walnuts, chia seeds, and flaxseeds are just a few examples of nutrient-rich options that can enhance our meals. While some nuts, like almonds, require significant water resources to grow, choosing those from sustainable sources or opting for varieties with lower water footprints, such as hazelnuts or sunflower seeds, can mitigate environmental impact. Additionally, many seeds can be grown in diverse climates, supporting agricultural biodiversity.

Sustainable seafood choices are critical for reducing the impact of overfishing and preserving marine ecosystems. The Monterey Bay Aquarium's Seafood Watch program provides guidelines on which seafood options are the most sustainable based on current fishing and farming practices. Opting for sustainably sourced fish, such as wild-caught Alaskan salmon or farmed shellfish, can help protect ocean health. Avoiding overfished species and supporting responsible aquaculture practices ensures that we can enjoy seafood without compromising marine biodiversity.

Herbs and spices play a crucial role in sustainable cooking by adding flavor and nutritional benefits without the need for artificial additives. Many herbs, such as basil, cilantro, and rosemary, can be grown at home, even in small spaces like windowsills or balconies. This not only ensures a fresh supply but also reduces the carbon footprint associated with transporting packaged herbs. Spices like turmeric, cinnamon, and cumin, when sourced from fair-trade and organic suppliers, can enhance dishes while supporting sustainable agricultural practices and fair labor conditions.

Dairy and meat alternatives are becoming increasingly popular as people seek to reduce their environmental impact. Plant-based milks, such as almond, oat, and soy milk, have a lower carbon and water footprint compared to dairy milk. When choosing plant-based milks, it is important to consider the sustainability of their production. For example, oat milk generally requires fewer resources than almond milk. Similarly, plant-based meat alternatives like tofu, tempeh, and seitan offer protein-rich options that are less resource-intensive than conventional meat. Incorporating these alternatives into our diets can significantly reduce our ecological footprint.

Fermented foods are another sustainable ingredient that can enhance both flavor and nutrition. Foods like sauerkraut, kimchi, miso, and yogurt are rich in probiotics, which support gut health. Fermentation is a preservation method that extends the shelf life of produce, reducing food waste. Many fermented foods can be made at home with simple ingredients, further promoting sustainability by reducing packaging waste and transportation emissions.

Sustainable oils and fats are essential for cooking and baking. Choosing oils like olive oil, avocado oil, and coconut oil from sustainable sources supports environmentally friendly agricultural practices. For instance, olive oil produced through traditional, organic methods is less resource-intensive than some industrially produced vegetable oils. Additionally, using these oils in moderation and exploring alternatives like nut butters or avocado in recipes can diversify our nutrient intake and support sustainable consumption.

Sweeteners are often overlooked in discussions of sustainable ingredients, but their impact is significant. Refined sugars have a high environmental footprint due to the intensive processing they require. Alternatives like honey, maple syrup, and coconut sugar can be more sustainable choices when sourced responsibly. For example, choosing honey from local, organic beekeepers supports sustainable beekeeping practices and biodiversity. Using sweeteners in moderation and exploring natural alternatives can reduce our reliance on highly processed sugars.

Finally, mindful consumption and waste reduction are integral to sustainable cooking. Planning meals, storing food properly, and using leftovers creatively can minimize food waste. Composting food scraps turns waste into valuable nutrients for gardens, closing the loop on the food cycle. By being conscious of portion sizes and avoiding over-purchasing, we can ensure that the food we bring into our homes is used fully and appreciated.

Bulk Buying and Storage Solutions

Bulk buying and proper storage solutions can transform how we manage our kitchens, save money, and reduce waste. The idea of purchasing in large quantities often brings images of overflowing pantries and excessive consumption, but when approached with a strategic mindset, it can be one of the most sustainable and economical methods of managing household provisions. The key lies in understanding how to buy, store, and use bulk items effectively.

The first step in bulk buying is to identify non-perishable and high-use items that make sense to purchase in larger quantities. Staples such as grains, beans, pasta, nuts, seeds, and dried fruits are excellent candidates. By buying these items in bulk, you can often get them at a lower price per unit, which can be a significant cost saving over time. For instance, purchasing a 10-pound bag of rice is typically cheaper per pound than buying smaller, one-pound packages. Additionally, bulk buying reduces the amount of packaging waste, as fewer individual packages are needed.

Once you've identified what to buy in bulk, it's crucial to have a plan for storing these items to maintain their quality and prevent spoilage. Proper storage solutions are essential to extend the shelf life of bulk goods. For dry goods like grains, beans, and pasta, airtight containers are a must. These containers protect the food from moisture, pests, and air exposure, which can lead to spoilage. Glass jars, plastic bins, and metal containers with tight-fitting lids are all good options. Clear containers are particularly useful because they allow you to see what's inside and how much is left, making inventory management easier.

For those with limited storage space, creative solutions can help. Consider using stackable containers to maximize vertical space in your pantry. Under-bed storage bins can be repurposed to hold bulk items, and hanging racks on pantry doors can provide additional storage for smaller containers. Labeling containers with the contents and purchase date ensures you use older items first, reducing the risk of food waste.

In addition to dry goods, bulk buying can extend to fresh produce, meats, and dairy products, provided you have the appropriate storage capabilities. Many fruits and vegetables can be purchased in bulk when they are in season and then preserved for later use. Freezing is a popular method; for example, buying a large quantity of berries when they are abundant and freezing them allows you to enjoy their flavor year-round. Blanching vegetables before freezing helps preserve their color, texture, and nutritional value.

Canning is another excellent way to store bulk produce. This method involves processing fruits and vegetables in jars at high temperatures to kill bacteria and create a vacuum seal, which can keep the contents shelf-stable for years. Homemade jams, pickles, and sauces made from bulk-bought produce not only reduce waste but also provide a sense of accomplishment and control over the ingredients in your food.

Meat and dairy products can also be purchased in bulk and stored effectively with the right approach. If you have a large freezer, buying meat in bulk cuts or even a share of a local farm animal can be cost-effective and ensure a steady supply. Portioning the meat into meal-sized servings and vacuum sealing them before freezing can prevent freezer burn and make meal preparation more convenient. For dairy, consider buying larger quantities of cheese and butter, which can be frozen for extended storage. Hard cheeses freeze well and can be grated directly from the freezer as needed.

A significant advantage of bulk buying is the ability to take advantage of sales and discounts. Stocking up on non-perishable items during sales can lead to substantial savings over time. However, it's important to avoid the temptation to buy more than you can realistically store or use before the items go bad. Developing a system to track your inventory and consumption patterns can help you make informed decisions about how much to buy and when.

When storing bulk items, it's also essential to consider the environment. A cool, dark, and dry place is ideal for most dry goods, as heat, light, and moisture can accelerate spoilage. Basements, pantries, and cupboards away from heat sources like stoves and ovens are typically good storage spots. For those living in smaller spaces, getting creative with storage solutions, such as utilizing closet space or installing additional shelving, can make bulk buying more feasible.

Another valuable strategy is to share bulk purchases with friends or neighbors. This approach allows you to enjoy the cost savings and environmental benefits of bulk buying without the need to store large quantities yourself. Cooperative buying not only fosters a sense of community but also ensures that food is used while it's still fresh.

Implementing a system for regularly rotating stock can prevent food from going to waste. The first-in, first-out (FIFO) method is a simple yet effective approach: always use the oldest items first and place newly purchased goods behind them. This practice ensures that nothing is forgotten at the back of the pantry and reduces the risk of spoilage.

It's also worth noting that bulk buying isn't limited to food items. Household essentials like cleaning supplies, toiletries, and paper products can also be purchased in larger quantities, often at a discount. Storing these items properly—such as keeping paper products in a dry area and cleaning supplies in a cool, ventilated space—can ensure they remain effective and ready for use.

To make the most of bulk buying, meal planning is an invaluable tool. Planning meals around the bulk items you have on hand can help reduce food waste and streamline grocery shopping. For example, if you've purchased a large bag of quinoa, you might plan several meals that incorporate it, such as salads, soups, and side dishes. This approach not only maximizes the use of your bulk purchases but also encourages creativity in the kitchen.

Understanding Labels: Organic, Fair Trade, and More

Navigating the vast array of labels on food products can be daunting, especially with terms like "organic," "fair trade," and others vying for attention. Understanding these labels is crucial for making informed choices that align with your values, whether they pertain to health, sustainability, or social justice. This chapter delves into the meaning behind these labels, demystifying the terms and explaining their significance.

Organic labels are perhaps the most well-known and widely discussed. At its core, organic farming emphasizes the use of natural substances and processes. In the United States, the USDA Organic label signifies that a product meets strict guidelines set by the Department of Agriculture. These regulations prohibit the use of most synthetic pesticides and fertilizers, genetic engineering, and ionizing radiation. Organic farming practices aim to enhance soil and water quality, reduce pollution, and promote a self-sustaining cycle of resources on a farm. When you see a USDA Organic label, it means the product is made with at least 95% organic ingredients, with the remaining 5% being non-organic substances approved by the USDA.

However, the term "organic" can sometimes be misleading due to variations in certification standards worldwide. For example, the European Union has its own organic certification system, which shares many similarities with the USDA's but also has distinct differences. Therefore, understanding the specific criteria of organic labels in your region or the region where the product is sourced is essential for truly comprehending what you're purchasing.

Fair Trade labels address a different aspect of food production, focusing on the economic and social conditions under which goods are produced. The Fair Trade certification ensures that farmers and workers receive fair wages, work in safe conditions, and engage in environmentally sustainable practices. Fair Trade standards also prohibit child labor and forced labor. By purchasing Fair Trade products, consumers support more equitable trading conditions and contribute to the improvement of living standards for producers in developing countries.

There are several organizations that certify Fair Trade products, such as Fairtrade International and Fair Trade USA. Each has its own set of standards and criteria, but the overarching goal remains the same: to promote fairness and sustainability in global trade. Fair Trade labels can be found on a variety of products, from coffee and chocolate to bananas and cotton. When you choose Fair Trade, you are not just buying a product; you are supporting a movement towards greater equity and sustainability in global supply chains.

Another important label to understand is the Rainforest Alliance Certified seal. This certification focuses on conserving biodiversity and ensuring sustainable livelihoods by transforming land-use practices, business practices, and consumer behavior. Products that carry the Rainforest Alliance Certified seal must meet rigorous environmental, social, and economic criteria, which are designed to protect ecosystems and the people and wildlife that depend on them. The certification applies to a wide range of products, including coffee, tea, bananas, and cocoa.

Non-GMO Project Verified is another label that has gained prominence, particularly among consumers concerned about genetically modified organisms (GMOs). The Non-GMO Project is a non-profit organization that offers third-party verification and labeling for non-GMO food and products. The label indicates that the product has been produced according to rigorous best practices for GMO avoidance, including testing of risk ingredients. While the debate over the safety and environmental impact of GMOs continues, this label provides a choice for consumers who prefer to avoid genetically modified ingredients in their food.

Whole Foods Market's Responsibly Grown rating system is an example of a retailer-specific label that evaluates produce and flowers on a variety of sustainability factors. The system rates products as "Good," "Better," or "Best" based on criteria such as pest management, farmworker welfare, and water conservation. This label helps consumers make more informed choices about the environmental and social impacts of their purchases, even within a single store.

Other labels focus on animal welfare, such as Certified Humane and Animal Welfare Approved. These certifications ensure that animals are raised in environments where they can engage in natural behaviors, have access to clean water and a nutritious diet, and are not subjected to unnecessary stress or suffering. The Certified Humane label, for instance, requires that animals are not confined in cages, crates, or tie stalls, and that they are provided with ample space, shelter, and gentle handling to limit stress. Animal Welfare Approved goes even further, with stringent standards that include pasture-based farming and independent annual audits to ensure compliance.

Understanding seafood labels can be particularly challenging due to the complexities of marine ecosystems and fishing practices. The Marine Stewardship Council (MSC) and Aquaculture Stewardship Council (ASC) are two prominent organizations that certify sustainable seafood. The MSC label indicates that a wild-caught seafood product comes from a fishery that meets rigorous standards for sustainable fishing, ensuring that fish stocks are maintained and the marine environment is protected. The ASC label, on the other hand, applies to farmed seafood and ensures that aquaculture operations minimize their environmental and social impacts.

Beyond these well-known labels, there are numerous other certifications and claims that can appear on food products. For example, the Gluten-Free Certification Organization (GFCO) provides certification for products that meet stringent gluten-free standards, which is crucial for individuals with celiac disease or gluten sensitivities. Similarly, the Certified Vegan label indicates that a product contains no animal ingredients or by-products and has not been tested on animals, catering to consumers who adhere to a vegan lifestyle.

Understanding these labels requires a certain level of diligence and sometimes even skepticism, as marketing tactics can sometimes blur the lines of what these certifications truly represent. It's important to research and familiarize yourself with the standards behind each label to ensure they align with your values and expectations.

Additionally, some labels are more trustworthy than others due to the rigor and transparency of their certification processes. Third-party certifications, where an independent organization evaluates and verifies compliance with specific standards, generally offer more credibility than self-declared claims by manufacturers. For example, the USDA Organic, Fair Trade, and Rainforest Alliance certifications involve thorough inspections and audits to ensure adherence to their respective standards.

In contrast, terms like "natural" or "eco-friendly" are often not regulated and can be used by manufacturers without meeting any specific criteria. These terms can be misleading, giving the impression of sustainability or health benefits without any substantial backing. Therefore, being an informed consumer involves looking beyond the marketing buzzwords and seeking out verified, reliable labels.

Being conscious of these labels empowers you to make choices that reflect your personal values, whether those are related to environmental sustainability, social justice, or health. By understanding what each label stands for, you can navigate the grocery store with confidence, selecting products that contribute to a better world.

Reducing Single-Use Plastics

The ubiquitous presence of single-use plastics in our daily lives has become an environmental crisis, with devastating impacts on ecosystems, wildlife, and human health. Reducing our reliance on these disposable items is crucial for mitigating pollution and fostering sustainable living. The journey towards minimizing single-use plastics begins with awareness and small, actionable steps that can collectively make a significant difference.

Single-use plastics are items designed to be used once and then discarded, often ending up in landfills or, worse, in our oceans. These include plastic bags, straws, bottles, cutlery, and packaging. The convenience they offer comes at a high environmental cost. For instance, a plastic bottle can take up to 450 years to decompose, during which time it can break down into microplastics that contaminate the soil and waterways, entering the food chain and potentially harming human health.

One of the most effective ways to reduce single-use plastics is to start with simple swaps in our daily routines. Consider the plastic bag—a staple in grocery stores worldwide. By switching to reusable cloth bags, you can significantly cut down on plastic waste. Many stores now offer incentives for bringing your own bags, making this an easy and cost-effective change. Similarly, opting for reusable produce bags instead of the thin plastic ones provided at supermarkets can further reduce your plastic footprint.

Water bottles are another major source of single-use plastic waste. Investing in a high-quality reusable water bottle can save hundreds of plastic bottles from being discarded each year. Many workplaces, gyms, and public places provide water fountains or refill stations, making it convenient to keep your bottle topped up throughout the day. Not only does this reduce plastic waste, but it also encourages better hydration habits.

Food packaging is another major contributor to plastic pollution. When shopping for groceries, choose products with minimal or no plastic packaging. Bulk stores offer a great alternative, allowing you to buy only what you need and often using your own containers. For items that do come in plastic, consider the packaging's recyclability and opt for those that can be easily processed by your local recycling program.

Dining out and takeout meals also present opportunities to cut down on single-use plastics. Bringing your own containers for leftovers or takeout can make a substantial difference. Some restaurants and cafes even offer discounts for customers who bring their own containers and cups. Additionally, carrying your own set of reusable cutlery and a metal straw can help eliminate the need for plastic utensils and straws provided by many eateries.

At home, there are numerous ways to reduce reliance on single-use plastics. Switching to bar soap and shampoo bars instead of liquid versions in plastic bottles can greatly diminish bathroom plastic waste. In the kitchen, using beeswax wraps or silicone lids instead of plastic wrap can help keep food fresh without the need for disposable plastics. Additionally, glass or stainless steel food storage containers are excellent alternatives to plastic ones, offering durability and safety for both you and the environment.

For those who enjoy gardening, there are creative ways to cut down on plastic use. Starting seeds in biodegradable pots or using natural materials like coconut coir instead of plastic trays can reduce plastic waste. Additionally, composting kitchen scraps can produce nutrient-rich soil without the need for plastic fertilizer bags.

Beyond individual actions, advocating for systemic change is crucial for addressing the plastic problem on a larger scale. Supporting legislation that restricts the use of single-use plastics and promotes sustainable alternatives can drive significant change. Many cities and countries have implemented bans or taxes on plastic bags, straws, and other disposable items, leading to a noticeable reduction in plastic waste. By voicing your support for such measures and encouraging others to do the same, you can help create a ripple effect that extends beyond your immediate community.

Education and outreach are also powerful tools in the fight against single-use plastics. Organizing or participating in community clean-up events can raise awareness about the extent of plastic pollution and inspire others to take action. Schools and workplaces can implement programs to reduce plastic use and promote sustainable practices, creating a culture of environmental stewardship.

Businesses play a critical role in reducing single-use plastics as well. Companies that prioritize sustainable packaging and operations can set a positive example and influence industry standards. As consumers, we can support these businesses by choosing products that align with our values and encouraging others to do the same. Many companies are now exploring innovative materials and designs to replace traditional plastics, such as biodegradable packaging made from plant-based materials or reusable containers that can be returned and refilled.

The fashion industry, too, can contribute to reducing plastic waste. Many clothing items contain synthetic fibers like polyester, which shed microplastics during washing. Opting for natural fibers, supporting brands that use recycled materials, and washing clothes less frequently and with full loads can help mitigate this issue.

Recycling, while not the ultimate solution, remains an important component of reducing plastic waste. Properly sorting and cleaning recyclables ensures that they can be effectively processed and repurposed. However, it's crucial to recognize that not all plastics are recyclable, and even those that are often have a limited recycling life. Therefore, reducing consumption and reusing items where possible should always be the primary focus.

The global nature of the plastic pollution problem requires coordinated efforts across borders. International agreements and collaborations can amplify the impact of local actions and address the issue at its source. Supporting organizations and initiatives that work towards global solutions can help drive the systemic changes needed to tackle plastic pollution on a larger scale.

The journey to reducing single-use plastics is ongoing and requires continuous effort and adaptation. By making conscious choices in our daily lives, advocating for systemic change, and supporting businesses and initiatives that prioritize sustainability, we can collectively reduce our dependence on disposable plastics. Every small action contributes to a larger movement towards a cleaner, healthier planet.

As we move forward, it's essential to remain informed and proactive. New technologies and solutions are constantly emerging, offering fresh opportunities to reduce plastic waste. Staying engaged with the latest developments and sharing knowledge with others can help maintain momentum and inspire broader participation in the fight against single-use plastics.

Homemade Alternatives to Store-Bought Staples

The allure of homemade alternatives to store-bought staples lies in the combination of cost savings, environmental benefits, and the joy of crafting something with your own hands. Creating your own household and pantry essentials can be both an empowering and satisfying endeavor, allowing you to tailor products to your specific preferences while reducing your reliance on commercial goods.

Consider the humble loaf of bread. Store-bought bread often contains preservatives and additives to extend shelf life—ingredients that can be avoided with homemade bread. Baking bread at home allows you to control the ingredients, from the type of flour to the inclusion of seeds and grains. The process of kneading dough and watching it rise can be therapeutic, and the aroma of freshly baked bread filling your home is a delight in itself. Plus, homemade bread tends to be more nutritious and flavorful than its store-bought counterparts.

Next, let's talk about cleaning products. Many commercial cleaners are laden with harsh chemicals that can be harmful to your health and the environment. Simple homemade alternatives can be just as effective. For instance, a mixture of vinegar and water can clean windows and surfaces, while baking soda and lemon juice can tackle stubborn stains and odors. Essential oils such as tea tree or lavender can add a pleasant scent and provide additional antibacterial properties. By making your own cleaning solutions, you can ensure they are safe for your family and the planet, and often at a fraction of the cost.

In the realm of personal care, homemade alternatives offer similar benefits. Take deodorant, for example. Many store-bought deodorants contain aluminum and other chemicals that some people prefer to avoid. A simple homemade deodorant can be made with coconut oil, baking soda, and essential oils. This natural alternative is gentle on the skin and can be customized with your favorite scents. Similarly, you can create your own toothpaste using ingredients like baking soda, coconut oil, and peppermint oil, avoiding the artificial sweeteners and preservatives found in many commercial brands.

Homemade beauty products are another area ripe for exploration. Face masks, scrubs, and lotions can be made with natural ingredients such as honey, oats, and avocado. These DIY beauty treatments can be tailored to your skin type and preferences, providing a luxurious and personalized experience. For example, a simple honey and oatmeal face mask can soothe and moisturize the skin, while a sugar and olive oil scrub can exfoliate and soften.

In the kitchen, homemade staples can enhance your culinary creations and reduce packaging waste. Making your own yogurt, for instance, is a straightforward process that yields delicious results. By simply heating milk, adding a yogurt starter, and letting it ferment, you can produce creamy, tangy yogurt with no added sugars or artificial ingredients. Homemade yogurt can be enjoyed on its own, used in recipes, or flavored with fresh fruit and honey.

Another versatile kitchen staple is broth. Homemade vegetable, chicken, or beef broth can be made by simmering scraps and bones with water and seasonings. This not only reduces food waste but also provides a flavorful base for soups, stews, and sauces. Homemade broth is often richer and more nutritious than store-bought versions, and it can be frozen in portions for easy use in future meals.

Homemade condiments can also elevate your dishes. Ketchup, mustard, and mayonnaise can all be made from scratch with simple ingredients. Homemade ketchup, for example, can be made with tomatoes, vinegar, and spices, allowing you to adjust the sweetness and spice to your liking. Similarly, homemade mayonnaise, made with egg yolks, oil, and lemon juice, is fresher and free from preservatives.

For those with a sweet tooth, homemade snacks and treats can be a healthier and more satisfying option. Granola bars, cookies, and even ice cream can be made at home with wholesome ingredients. Homemade granola bars, for instance, can be packed with nuts, seeds, and dried fruit, providing a nutritious and energy-boosting snack. Making your own cookies allows you to control the sugar content and use natural sweeteners like honey or maple syrup. Homemade ice cream, made with real cream and fresh fruit, is a delightful treat that can be customized with endless flavor combinations.

In addition to food and personal care products, homemade alternatives can extend to household items. Cloth napkins, for example, can replace disposable paper ones, reducing waste and adding a touch of elegance to your meals. These can be made from old fabric scraps or purchased materials, and they can be easily washed and reused. Similarly, reusable kitchen sponges and cleaning cloths can be made from old towels or fabric, cutting down on disposable sponge waste.

Crafting your own candles and soaps can also be a rewarding experience. Homemade candles, made with beeswax or soy wax and scented with essential oils, provide a natural and cozy ambiance without the synthetic fragrances found in many store-bought candles. Homemade soap, made with oils, lye, and natural additives like herbs and oatmeal, can be tailored to your skin's needs and preferences.

The benefits of homemade alternatives extend beyond the products themselves. Engaging in these DIY projects can foster a sense of accomplishment and creativity. It can also be a great way to involve family and friends, turning the process into a fun and educational activity. Children, in particular, can learn valuable skills and gain an appreciation for the effort that goes into making everyday items.

Moreover, homemade alternatives often result in cost savings. While there may be an initial investment in ingredients or equipment, the long-term savings can be substantial. For example, the cost of ingredients for homemade cleaning products is typically much lower than purchasing commercial cleaners. Similarly, making your own bread, yogurt, and other staples can be more economical than buying them pre-made.

Reducing reliance on store-bought staples by making your own at home also contributes to a more sustainable lifestyle. It reduces packaging waste, minimizes exposure to harmful chemicals, and supports a more self-sufficient way of living. By taking control of what goes into the products you use, you can make healthier choices for yourself and your family while also lessening your environmental impact.

Chapter 3

Seasonal Cooking

The Benefits of Eating Seasonally

Eating seasonally is more than just a trend; it's a practice deeply rooted in centuries of tradition. Our ancestors, without the luxury of modern transportation and refrigeration, naturally ate what was available during each season. Today, though we have access to a vast array of food year-round, there are compelling reasons to return to the practice of eating seasonally.

The first and perhaps most obvious benefit of eating seasonally is the superior taste and quality of the produce. Fruits and vegetables that are in season are allowed to ripen naturally, which enhances their flavor. Think of a vine-ripened tomato picked at the peak of summer, bursting with sweet, tangy juice, compared to a pale, mealy supermarket tomato available in the dead of winter. The seasonal tomato, having been harvested at the right time, offers a taste experience that is hard to match.

Nutritional benefits are another significant advantage of eating seasonally. Produce that is harvested in its prime retains more nutrients than those that are grown out of season and transported long distances. For example, leafy greens like spinach and kale, which are abundant in spring and fall, are packed with vitamins A, C, and K, as well as folate and iron. When these greens are consumed fresh and in season, their nutrient content is at its highest, providing more health benefits.

Seasonal eating also supports local agriculture and the economy. By purchasing produce from local farmers, you are helping to sustain their livelihoods and encouraging the growth of your local food system. This, in turn, reduces the carbon footprint associated with transporting food over long distances. When you buy from local markets, you also often get the opportunity to learn about the farming practices used and develop a connection with the people who grow your food.

Environmental sustainability is another key benefit of eating seasonally. Growing produce out of season typically requires more resources, such as energy for heating greenhouses and water for irrigation. Seasonal crops are naturally adapted to the local climate, requiring fewer artificial inputs. This makes seasonal farming more environmentally friendly and reduces the overall impact on the planet.

Cost savings is an often-overlooked advantage of seasonal eating. When produce is in season, it is usually more abundant and, therefore, less expensive. Conversely, out-of-season fruits and vegetables can be significantly pricier due to the costs associated with importing and storing them. By aligning your diet with the seasons, you can enjoy a variety of fresh, affordable produce throughout the year.

Eating seasonally also encourages a more varied and balanced diet. Each season brings a different assortment of fruits and vegetables, prompting you to diversify your meals and try new recipes. This variety ensures that you consume a wide range of nutrients, which is essential for maintaining good health. For example, summer might bring an abundance of berries, tomatoes, and zucchini, while autumn offers pumpkins, apples, and Brussels sprouts. By rotating your diet with the seasons, you can enjoy the nutritional benefits of a broad spectrum of produce.

There's also a profound connection to nature and the rhythm of the seasons that comes from eating seasonally. This practice fosters a greater appreciation for the natural world and its cycles. As you become more attuned to the seasons, you might find yourself looking forward to the first strawberries of summer or the hearty root vegetables of winter. This connection to nature can enhance your overall well-being and mindfulness about where your food comes from.

Preparing meals with seasonal ingredients can also be a source of culinary inspiration and creativity. Seasonal produce often brings unique flavors and textures that can elevate your cooking. For instance, springtime asparagus can be roasted, grilled, or added to a fresh salad, while fall's butternut squash can be transformed into a creamy soup or a satisfying roasted side dish. By focusing on what's in season, you can explore new recipes and cooking techniques, making your meals more exciting and enjoyable.

In addition to the direct benefits of eating seasonally, there are broader societal impacts to consider. When communities embrace seasonal eating, there is a collective shift towards sustainable food practices. This can lead to increased demand for local, seasonal produce, encouraging more farmers to adopt sustainable farming methods. Over time, this can contribute to a more resilient and sustainable food system.

To get started with eating seasonally, it's helpful to familiarize yourself with the seasonal produce calendar for your region. Local farmers' markets are great places to see what's currently in season and to ask farmers for recommendations. Many markets even offer seasonal guides or recipe ideas to help you make the most of the produce available.

Another practical tip is to join a Community Supported Agriculture (CSA) program. CSA programs allow you to purchase a share of a local farm's harvest, receiving a box of fresh produce on a regular basis. This not only guarantees you a variety of seasonal produce but also gives you the opportunity to support local farmers directly. Participating in a CSA can be a fun and convenient way to incorporate seasonal eating into your lifestyle.

Storing and preserving seasonal produce is another way to extend the benefits of seasonal eating throughout the year. Techniques such as canning, freezing, and drying can help you enjoy the taste and nutrition of seasonal fruits and vegetables long after their peak season has passed. For example, canning tomatoes in the summer can provide you with flavorful, homemade tomato sauce during the winter months. Freezing berries allows you to enjoy their sweetness in smoothies and desserts year-round.

For those with a bit of space and a green thumb, growing your own seasonal produce can be an incredibly rewarding experience. Home gardening allows you to cultivate your favorite seasonal fruits and vegetables right in your backyard or even on a balcony. This not only provides fresh, homegrown food but also deepens your connection to the growing cycles and the effort required to produce food.

Ultimately, eating seasonally is about making conscious choices that benefit your health, your community, and the environment. It's a practice that encourages mindfulness, sustainability, and a greater appreciation for the food we eat. By embracing the rhythms of the seasons, you can enjoy fresher, more flavorful produce while supporting local farmers and reducing your ecological footprint.

Incorporating seasonal eating into your lifestyle doesn't have to be an all-or-nothing approach. Start by making small changes, such as choosing seasonal fruits and vegetables when grocery shopping or visiting a farmers' market once a week. Over time, these small steps can lead to a more profound shift in your eating habits and a greater connection to the natural world.

Seasonal Produce Guide

Navigating the world of seasonal produce can transform your culinary experience, connecting you more intimately with the rhythms of nature and the flavors of each season. A seasonal produce guide serves as a roadmap, helping you to select the freshest, most flavorful fruits and vegetables throughout the year. Understanding what's in season not only enhances the taste of your meals but also supports local farmers and promotes sustainability.

Spring ushers in a bounty of fresh, vibrant produce as the earth begins to awaken from its winter slumber. As the chill of winter fades and the days grow longer, farmers markets and grocery stores start to brim with early greens and tender vegetables. Look for asparagus, whose tender stalks are perfect for grilling or roasting. Peas, whether snap, snow, or English, bring a sweet, crisp addition to salads and stir-fries. Spring also heralds the arrival of radishes, their peppery bite adding a refreshing crunch to dishes. Leafy greens such as spinach, arugula, and lettuces are at their peak, offering a wealth of vitamins and minerals. Strawberries, with their juicy sweetness, make their first appearance, ideal for desserts or simply enjoyed fresh.

As spring transitions into summer, the produce options expand dramatically, reflecting the season's warmth and abundance. Farmers markets overflow with colorful, nutrient-rich fruits and vegetables. Tomatoes, perhaps the quintessential summer produce, burst with flavor, whether eaten fresh, made into sauces, or roasted. Cucumbers provide a cooling counterpoint in salads and pickles. Zucchini and summer squash are versatile, excellent for grilling, baking, or incorporating into casseroles. Sweet corn, with its golden kernels, is a summer staple, perfect boiled, grilled, or even raw in salads. Bell peppers, in a spectrum of colors, add crunch and sweetness to a variety of dishes. Fruits such as blueberries, raspberries, blackberries, and peaches are at their peak, offering natural sweetness for snacks, desserts, or preserving.

Fall brings a shift in the produce landscape, with heartier vegetables and fruits that reflect the season's cooler temperatures and shorter days. Root vegetables like carrots, beets, and turnips are plentiful, their earthy flavors deepening with roasting or stewing. Squash varieties, including butternut, acorn, and delicata, become central to comforting fall dishes, from soups to roasted sides. Apples, available in countless varieties, offer versatility for both sweet and savory recipes, from pies to salads to sauces. Pears, too, make their appearance, their delicate sweetness ideal for baking or poaching. Brussels sprouts and cauliflower, their flavors enhanced by roasting, become prominent in fall meals. Pumpkins, beyond their role in holiday pies, provide a rich base for soups and breads.

Winter may seem a challenging time for fresh produce, but a surprising variety of fruits and vegetables thrive in the colder months. Root vegetables continue to be staples, with parsnips, rutabagas, and sweet potatoes offering robust flavors and nutrients. Hardy greens such as kale and collard greens withstand the frost, becoming sweeter with cold exposure. Citrus fruits like oranges, grapefruits, and lemons reach their peak, bringing bright, tangy flavors and a dose of vitamin C. Winter squash, including spaghetti squash and kabocha, provide hearty bases for meals. Pomegranates, with their jewel-like seeds, add a burst of tartness to salads and desserts. Cabbage and leeks, often overlooked, become stars in winter stews and sautés, offering depth and warmth.

Knowing what's in season is not merely about availability; it's also about maximizing flavor and nutrition. Seasonal produce is harvested at its peak, ensuring the highest levels of vitamins, minerals, and antioxidants. For example, tomatoes ripened on the vine in summer contain more lycopene, a powerful antioxidant, compared to those grown in hothouses during the winter. Similarly, leafy greens like kale and spinach are packed with nutrients when harvested in their natural growing seasons. Consuming seasonal produce supports your health by providing a rotation of nutrients tailored to the body's needs throughout the year.

Shopping for seasonal produce encourages visits to farmers markets or participation in Community Supported Agriculture (CSA) programs. These avenues not only provide access to the freshest produce but also foster a connection with local farmers and the land. Farmers markets offer a sensory experience, with the sights, smells, and tastes of fresh produce creating a deeper appreciation for the food on your plate. CSAs provide a direct link to the farming process, often including newsletters or farm visits that educate about sustainable practices and seasonal cycles.

To make the most of seasonal produce, consider cooking methods that highlight their natural flavors. Simple preparations such as roasting, grilling, or steaming often suffice, allowing the inherent taste of the produce to shine. For instance, roasting root vegetables with a drizzle of olive oil and a sprinkle of sea salt caramelizes their sugars, enhancing their natural sweetness. Grilling summer vegetables like zucchini and peppers imparts a smoky depth that complements their fresh flavors. Steaming greens like spinach and kale preserves their nutrients while providing a tender texture.

Preserving the bounty of each season is another way to enjoy seasonal produce year-round. Techniques such as canning, freezing, and drying allow you to capture the peak flavors and nutrition of fruits and vegetables. Canning tomatoes in summer, for instance, ensures a supply of rich, homemade sauces during the winter months. Freezing berries at their ripest preserves their sweetness for smoothies or baking. Drying herbs and fruits extends their shelf life, providing a taste of summer even in the depths of winter.

Incorporating seasonal produce into your diet doesn't have to be daunting. Start by familiarizing yourself with what's in season in your region, using resources such as local extension services, farmers markets, or online guides. Plan your meals around the seasonal offerings, experimenting with new recipes and cooking techniques. Over time, eating seasonally becomes second nature, a rhythm that aligns with the natural cycle of growth and harvest.

Eating seasonally offers more than just culinary rewards; it's a holistic approach that benefits your health, supports local agriculture, and promotes environmental sustainability. By choosing seasonal produce, you contribute to a food system that values freshness, nutrition, and ecological balance. The simple act of selecting fruits and vegetables in season can lead to a deeper connection with your food, your community, and the earth.

How to Preserve Seasonal Foods

Preserving seasonal foods extends the bounty of each harvest, allowing you to enjoy the flavors and nutrients of fresh produce year-round. This practice, rooted in tradition, offers a way to save money, reduce food waste, and maintain a connection to the rhythms of nature. With a variety of methods available, from canning and freezing to drying and fermenting, preserving seasonal foods can be both an art and a science, requiring a bit of practice and patience.

Canning is one of the most popular methods for preserving seasonal foods. This technique involves placing foods in jars and heating them to a temperature that destroys microorganisms and inactivates enzymes that could cause spoilage. There are two main types of canning: water bath canning and pressure canning. Water bath canning is suitable for high-acid foods like fruits, pickles, and tomatoes. The high acidity of these foods helps to prevent the growth of bacteria. On the other hand, low-acid foods such as vegetables, meats, and soups require pressure canning to reach the higher temperatures necessary to ensure safety. The process of canning not only preserves the food but also often enhances its flavor, as the ingredients meld together over time.

Freezing is another effective method for preserving seasonal foods. It involves lowering the temperature of food to inhibit the growth of microorganisms and slow down enzymatic reactions. Freezing is particularly well-suited for fruits and vegetables, which retain their flavor, color, and nutritional value when frozen properly. To freeze produce effectively, it's important to blanch vegetables first. Blanching, a brief boiling followed by rapid cooling, inactivates enzymes that can cause loss of flavor, color, and texture. Fruits, on the other hand, can often be frozen directly, though some benefit from a coating of sugar or syrup to maintain their texture and flavor. Proper packaging is crucial in freezing; use airtight containers or heavy-duty freezer bags to prevent freezer burn and maintain quality.

Drying is one of the oldest methods of food preservation, relying on the removal of moisture to inhibit the growth of microorganisms. This method can be used for a wide range of foods, including fruits, vegetables, herbs, and meats. Sun drying, oven drying, and using a food dehydrator are common techniques. Sun drying requires a hot, dry climate and can take several days, while oven drying and dehydrators offer more control and faster results. Dried foods are lightweight, compact, and can be stored at room temperature, making them ideal for long-term storage and easy transport. The key to successful drying is ensuring that the food is thoroughly dehydrated and then stored in a cool, dry place in airtight containers to keep it from reabsorbing moisture.

Fermentation is a unique method of preservation that not only extends the shelf life of foods but also enhances their nutritional value and flavor. This process relies on the action of beneficial bacteria and yeasts to convert sugars into acids, gases, or alcohol, which act as natural preservatives. Fermented foods such as sauerkraut, kimchi, yogurt, and kombucha are rich in probiotics, which support gut health. The process of fermentation can be simple, often requiring just salt, water, and time. For example, making sauerkraut involves shredding cabbage, mixing it with salt, and allowing it to ferment in a jar at room temperature for several weeks. The result is a tangy, crunchy condiment that can be enjoyed for months.

Pickling is a form of preservation that uses an acidic brine, typically vinegar-based, to inhibit the growth of spoilage organisms. Pickling can be done with a variety of vegetables and fruits, creating a range of textures and flavors from crisp cucumbers to spicy peppers. Quick pickling is a simple method that involves immersing produce in a hot vinegar brine and refrigerating it, resulting in tangy, flavorful pickles that can be enjoyed within a few days. Traditional pickling, which includes fermenting the produce in a saltwater brine, develops deeper flavors and can be stored for longer periods.

Proper storage conditions play a crucial role in the success of preserving seasonal foods. Each method has specific requirements to ensure the longevity and safety of the preserved food. For canned goods, store jars in a cool, dark place, and always check the seals before use to ensure they remain intact. Frozen foods should be kept at a constant temperature of 0°F (-18°C) or lower, and it's helpful to label packages with dates to use the oldest items first. Dried foods should be kept in airtight containers in a cool, dry place to prevent moisture reabsorption and spoilage. Fermented foods, once they reach the desired level of fermentation, should be stored in the refrigerator to slow down the fermentation process and extend shelf life. Pickled items can be stored in the refrigerator or a cool pantry, depending on the method used.

Beyond the practical aspects, preserving seasonal foods can become a source of joy and creativity in the kitchen. It allows you to experiment with flavors, textures, and techniques, transforming fresh produce into an array of delicious, long-lasting foods. Preserving can also be a social activity, bringing together family and friends to share in the process and the rewards. The act of preserving food connects us to traditions and cultures, offering a sense of continuity and a way to honor the labor and care that goes into growing and harvesting crops.

For beginners, starting with simple projects can build confidence and skills. Quick pickles, freezer jams, and dried herbs are excellent entry points, requiring minimal equipment and time. As you gain experience, you can venture into more complex methods like pressure canning or fermentation. Resources such as books, online tutorials, and local extension services can provide valuable guidance and support.

Preserving seasonal foods also aligns with sustainable living practices. It reduces reliance on commercially processed foods and their associated packaging, lowers food waste by extending the usability of fresh produce, and supports local agriculture. By preserving the harvest, you can enjoy the flavors of each season, reduce your environmental footprint, and contribute to a more resilient food system.

Incorporating preserved foods into your meals can be straightforward and rewarding. Home-canned tomatoes can serve as the base for soups and sauces, while frozen berries can be blended into smoothies or baked into desserts. Dried fruits and vegetables make convenient snacks and can be rehydrated for use in recipes. Fermented foods add probiotics and vibrant flavors to dishes, and pickled vegetables offer a tangy complement to sandwiches and salads.

Recipes for Every Season

Embracing the culinary potential of each season means more than simply enjoying what's fresh and available; it's about creating dishes that celebrate the unique flavors and textures of seasonal ingredients. From the tender greens of spring to the hearty roots of winter, every season offers distinct produce that can be transformed into delightful meals. Crafting recipes that highlight these seasonal ingredients not only enriches your culinary repertoire but also supports local agriculture and promotes sustainability.

Spring arrives with a burst of freshness, embodying renewal and growth. The markets brim with tender asparagus, sweet peas, and vibrant radishes. One delightful way to celebrate these ingredients is with a Spring Vegetable Risotto. Start by sautéing finely chopped onions and garlic in olive oil until translucent. Stir in Arborio rice, allowing it to toast slightly before gradually adding warm vegetable broth. As the rice absorbs the liquid, fold in blanched asparagus tips, fresh peas, and thinly sliced radishes. Finish with a generous handful of grated Parmesan and a squeeze of lemon juice to brighten the flavors. This creamy, vibrant dish captures the essence of spring, offering a perfect balance of tenderness and crunch.

As spring transitions to summer, the bounty multiplies. Tomatoes, zucchini, and berries take center stage, their flavors intensified by the sun. A classic Ratatouille is an excellent way to showcase summer's abundance. Begin by sautéing diced onions and garlic in olive oil until fragrant. Add chopped bell peppers, eggplants, and zucchinis, cooking until they start to soften. Stir in ripe, chopped tomatoes and simmer until the vegetables meld into a harmonious medley. Season with fresh thyme, rosemary, and a splash of balsamic vinegar. Serve this colorful, aromatic stew with crusty bread or as a side to grilled meats. Its rich, layered flavors encapsulate the peak of summer produce.

For a sweet summer treat, consider a Mixed Berry Tart. Start with a buttery, flaky crust as the base. Spread a layer of lemon-infused mascarpone cheese over the cooled crust. Arrange an assortment of fresh berries—strawberries, blueberries, raspberries—on top, creating a vibrant, jewel-toned mosaic. A light glaze of apricot jam melted with a bit of water adds a glistening finish. This tart not only tastes divine but also looks stunning, making it a perfect centerpiece for summer gatherings.

As the days shorten and the air cools, fall brings a different kind of harvest. Squash, pumpkins, and apples dominate the landscape, their flavors deep and comforting. A Butternut Squash Soup is a quintessential fall dish, warming and satisfying. Begin by roasting cubed butternut squash with olive oil, salt, and pepper until caramelized. Meanwhile, sauté onions, garlic, and a touch of ginger in a large pot. Add the roasted squash and enough vegetable broth to cover. Simmer until everything is tender, then blend until smooth. Stir in a splash of coconut milk for creaminess and finish with a sprinkle of nutmeg. This soup, with its velvety texture and rich, earthy flavors, is a perfect antidote to crisp autumn evenings.

For a hearty fall entrée, try a Mushroom and Barley Pilaf. Sauté a mix of wild mushrooms in butter until golden. Set aside and in the same pan, cook chopped onions, garlic, and carrots until soft. Add pearl barley and toast lightly before pouring in vegetable broth. Simmer until the barley is tender and has absorbed most of the liquid. Stir the mushrooms back in and season with fresh thyme and a splash of sherry vinegar. This dish, with its nutty barley and meaty mushrooms, is both nutritious and deeply satisfying, embodying the essence of autumn.

Winter's chill calls for hearty, robust dishes that provide warmth and comfort. Root vegetables like carrots, parsnips, and potatoes are at their peak. A classic Beef Stew makes excellent use of these ingredients. Begin by browning cubes of beef in a heavy pot. Remove the beef and sauté onions, garlic, and celery in the same pot. Add chunks of carrots, parsnips, and potatoes, stirring to coat with the flavorful fond. Return the beef to the pot and pour in red wine and beef broth. Add bay leaves, thyme, and a bit of tomato paste. Simmer slowly until the meat is tender and the vegetables are soft, creating a rich, hearty stew perfect for cold winter nights.

For a winter dessert, consider a Spiced Apple Cake. Cream together butter and sugar until light and fluffy.

Beat in eggs, then fold in flour, baking powder, and a mix of warm spices such as cinnamon, nutmeg, and cloves. Stir in grated apples and chopped walnuts. Bake until golden and a skewer inserted into the center comes out clean. This cake, with its moist texture and fragrant spices, is an ideal winter treat, evoking the cozy feel of the season.

Cooking with the seasons not only enhances the flavors of your dishes but also connects you to the natural world. Each season's ingredients offer unique culinary opportunities, encouraging creativity and experimentation in the kitchen. By focusing on what's fresh and local, you support sustainable farming practices and reduce your carbon footprint. Moreover, seasonal eating can be more affordable, as produce in season is often less expensive and more abundant.

Incorporating seasonal recipes into your meal planning can also provide nutritional benefits. Seasonal produce is typically harvested at its peak, meaning it's more likely to be nutrient-dense compared to out-of-season counterparts that may have traveled long distances. This freshness translates to better taste and health benefits, as the vitamins and minerals are more intact.

Beyond the practical and nutritional aspects, there's a certain joy in anticipating the different flavors each season brings. The first strawberries of spring, the tomatoes of summer, the apples of fall, and the hearty roots of winter each mark a new chapter in the culinary calendar. This rhythm of change keeps cooking exciting and varied, preventing the monotony that can come from eating the same foods year-round.

To integrate seasonal cooking into your routine, start by visiting local farmers' markets or joining a community-supported agriculture (CSA) program. These sources provide the freshest produce and often introduce you to varieties you might not find in supermarkets. Let the ingredients guide your menu planning, and don't be afraid to try new recipes or adapt old favorites to use seasonal ingredients.

Another way to embrace seasonal cooking is to preserve the flavors of each season. Techniques like canning, freezing, drying, and fermenting allow you to enjoy seasonal produce long after its harvest. For example, making jam from summer berries, pickling fall vegetables, or freezing winter greens can extend their availability and add variety to your meals throughout the year.

Cooking seasonally fosters a deeper appreciation for the food you eat and the effort required to grow it. It encourages mindfulness and gratitude, connecting you to the earth's cycles and the farmers who cultivate the land. It also creates opportunities for learning and growth in the kitchen, as you discover new ingredients and methods with each passing season.

Planning a Seasonal Menu

Creating a seasonal menu involves more than simply selecting ingredients at their peak freshness. It's about crafting a dining experience that reflects the natural rhythms of the year, celebrates the bounty of each season, and brings joy to both the cook and the diners. Planning such a menu requires a balance of creativity, knowledge, and practicality. By understanding the characteristics and availability of seasonal produce, you can design meals that are not only delicious but also visually appealing and nutritionally balanced.

Begin with the foundation of any great menu: fresh, seasonal ingredients. Spring, with its promise of renewal, offers tender greens, delicate herbs, and the first hints of fruit. Imagine a spring menu starting with a vibrant salad of mixed baby greens, adorned with thinly sliced radishes and dressed in a light lemon vinaigrette. Follow this with a main course featuring fresh peas and asparagus, perhaps in a creamy risotto or a simple pasta dish with a bright pesto sauce. For dessert, a rhubarb tart or strawberry shortcake can perfectly capture the essence of spring's sweet and tangy flavors.

As summer arrives, the market's offerings become even more abundant and colorful. Think of a summer menu beginning with a chilled gazpacho, made from ripe tomatoes, cucumbers, and bell peppers, all blended to create a refreshing starter. A grilled main course, such as marinated chicken or fish, pairs beautifully with a side of corn on the cob and a salad of heirloom tomatoes, basil, and mozzarella. Finish with a dessert that highlights the season's fruits, like a mixed berry cobbler or a peach galette, which can be served warm with a scoop of vanilla ice cream.

Autumn's arrival brings a shift to heartier, more comforting dishes. The richness of squash, root vegetables, and apples defines this season. Picture an autumn menu that starts with a roasted butternut squash soup, smooth and spiced with nutmeg and cinnamon. For the main course, consider a roast chicken served with a medley of roasted root vegetables—carrots, parsnips, and sweet potatoes—all caramelized to perfection. An apple crisp or a pumpkin pie offers a sweet, spiced conclusion to this meal, evoking the warmth and coziness of fall.

Winter demands even more robust and warming dishes to combat the cold. Think of a winter menu starting with a hearty lentil soup, full of earthy flavors and fortified with winter greens like kale. A slow-cooked beef stew or a rich mushroom risotto makes for an ideal main course, pairing well with sides of mashed potatoes or roasted Brussels sprouts. For dessert, a spiced gingerbread cake or a pear and almond tart can provide a sweet, comforting end to a winter feast.

Balancing flavors, textures, and colors is crucial when planning a seasonal menu. Each course should complement the others, creating a cohesive dining experience. Start with lighter, fresher flavors and gradually build to richer, more complex dishes. This progression mirrors the natural growth and maturation of seasonal produce. For example, a spring menu might progress from a light salad to a more substantial main course, while a winter menu might start with a hearty soup and move to an even richer stew.

Incorporating a variety of cooking techniques also enhances your seasonal menu. Roasting, grilling, steaming, and braising each bring out different qualities in seasonal ingredients. Roasting vegetables, for instance, concentrates their natural sugars and enhances their flavors, making them ideal for fall and winter dishes. Grilling is perfect for summer, imparting a smoky depth to meats and vegetables.

Steaming preserves the delicate flavors and textures of spring produce, while braising is excellent for creating rich, comforting dishes in the colder months.

Sourcing your ingredients locally not only ensures freshness but also supports local farmers and reduces your carbon footprint. Visit farmers' markets, farm stands, or join a CSA (Community Supported Agriculture) program to get the best of what each season has to offer. Building relationships with local growers can also provide you with insights into the most flavorful and interesting varieties of produce available.

In addition to selecting seasonal produce, consider how proteins and grains fit into your menu. Spring and summer call for lighter proteins such as chicken, fish, and plant-based options. In contrast, fall and winter are ideal for heartier meats like beef, lamb, and pork. Grains and legumes can provide an excellent base for seasonal dishes, adding texture and nutritional balance. Quinoa, farro, and barley are versatile choices that can be adapted to any season.

Presentation plays a significant role in the enjoyment of your seasonal menu. Take inspiration from the colors and shapes of your ingredients to create visually appealing dishes. In spring, use edible flowers and fresh herbs to garnish plates, adding a touch of elegance and freshness. Summer dishes can be vibrant and colorful, reflecting the abundance of the season. Fall and winter presentations can focus on warm, rich tones, using elements like roasted vegetables and dark greens to create a comforting, inviting look.

Planning a seasonal menu also involves considering dietary preferences and restrictions of your guests. Offering a variety of dishes, including vegetarian or gluten-free options, ensures that everyone can enjoy the meal. Seasonal ingredients often lend themselves well to these adaptations, as their natural flavors need minimal enhancement.

To ensure your seasonal menu is both practical and enjoyable to prepare, plan your cooking schedule carefully. Some dishes can be made ahead of time, allowing you to focus on more complex tasks closer to serving time. Soups, stews, and desserts often benefit from being prepared in advance, as their flavors meld and improve over time. Fresh salads and grilled items, on the other hand, are best prepared just before serving to retain their optimal texture and flavor.

Seasonal menus are not just about the food; they also create an opportunity to reflect on the changing seasons and celebrate the passing of time. Each menu marks a moment in the year, connecting you and your diners to the natural world. This connection enhances the dining experience, making it more meaningful and memorable.

Chapter 4

Plant-Based Eating

Introduction to Plant-Based Diets

A plant-based diet emphasizes foods derived from plants, including not only fruits and vegetables but also nuts, seeds, oils, whole grains, legumes, and beans. It does not necessarily mean that you are vegetarian or vegan and never eat meat or dairy. Rather, you are proportionately choosing more of your foods from plant sources. This dietary approach has gained significant popularity due to its numerous health benefits, environmental advantages, and ethical considerations.

One of the most compelling reasons to adopt a plant-based diet is its potential for improving overall health. Research consistently shows that plant-based diets are linked to lower risks of heart disease, high blood pressure, diabetes, and certain cancers. These diets are typically rich in fiber, vitamins, and antioxidants, which contribute to better health outcomes. For instance, a diet high in fruits and vegetables can provide essential nutrients like potassium, magnesium, and vitamins A, C, and K, which support bodily functions and protect against chronic diseases.

Fiber is a critical component of a plant-based diet. It aids in digestion, helps maintain a healthy weight, and reduces the risk of heart disease. Unlike animal-based foods, plant foods are naturally high in dietary fiber. Whole grains, legumes, vegetables, and fruits are excellent sources of both soluble and insoluble fiber. Soluble fiber, found in foods like oats and beans, can help lower blood cholesterol levels and stabilize blood sugar. Insoluble fiber, present in whole grains and vegetables, promotes regular bowel movements and prevents constipation.

Transitioning to a plant-based diet can also lead to weight loss and improved weight management. Plant-based foods are generally lower in calories and higher in fiber, which can help you feel full and satisfied with fewer calories. This can naturally lead to a reduction in calorie intake without the need for strict dieting or calorie counting. Studies have shown that individuals following plant-based diets tend to have lower body mass indexes (BMIs) compared to those who consume meat regularly.

In addition to health benefits, plant-based diets have a significantly lower environmental impact than diets high in animal products. The production of plant foods requires fewer resources such as land, water, and energy. For example, producing a kilogram of beef requires approximately 15,000 liters of water, whereas producing the same amount of vegetables requires only a fraction of that amount. Additionally, animal agriculture is a major contributor to greenhouse gas emissions, which drive climate change. By choosing plant-based foods, you can reduce your carbon footprint and contribute to environmental sustainability.

Ethical considerations also play a crucial role in the decision to adopt a plant-based diet. Many individuals choose this dietary approach to avoid contributing to animal suffering and exploitation. The conditions in which many animals are raised and slaughtered for food can be inhumane, and a plant-based diet eliminates the demand for such practices. This ethical standpoint is often tied to a broader philosophy of non-violence and respect for all living beings.

Starting a plant-based diet may seem daunting, but it can be a gradual process rather than an overnight change. Begin by incorporating more plant-based meals into your weekly routine. Experiment with new recipes and ingredients to discover what you enjoy. For breakfast, consider oatmeal topped with fresh fruit and nuts or a smoothie made with leafy greens, berries, and plant-based milk. Lunch could be a hearty salad with a variety of colorful vegetables, beans, and a whole grain like quinoa. For dinner, try dishes like vegetable stir-fries, lentil soups, or bean-based chili.

Protein is often a concern for those new to plant-based diets, but there are plenty of plant sources that can meet your needs. Legumes, such as beans, lentils, and chickpeas, are excellent sources of protein and can be used in a variety of dishes. Tofu and tempeh, made from soybeans, are versatile protein sources that can be marinated, grilled, or stir-fried. Nuts and seeds, including almonds, sunflower seeds, and chia seeds, also provide protein along with healthy fats. Whole grains like quinoa, farro, and bulgur contain more protein than refined grains and can be included in salads, soups, and side dishes.

It's important to ensure that your plant-based diet is balanced and includes a variety of foods to meet all your nutritional needs. While plant-based diets can provide all essential nutrients, some vitamins and minerals require special attention. Vitamin B12, for example, is primarily found in animal products, so individuals on a plant-based diet should consider fortified foods or supplements. Omega-3 fatty acids, important for heart and brain health, can be obtained from flaxseeds, chia seeds, and walnuts, or through algae-based supplements. Iron and calcium are also crucial nutrients that can be found in leafy greens, legumes, tofu, and fortified plant milks.

Cooking at home is one of the best ways to ensure you are eating a balanced plant-based diet. Preparing your meals allows you to control the ingredients and avoid hidden animal products or excessive added sugars and fats often found in processed foods. Experimenting with different cooking methods, such as roasting, steaming, and grilling, can help you discover new flavors and textures. Don't be afraid to try international cuisines that naturally incorporate plant-based foods, such as Indian, Mediterranean, and Mexican dishes.

Community support and education can be invaluable when transitioning to a plant-based diet. Joining local or online groups can provide you with resources, recipe ideas, and encouragement from like-minded individuals. Attending plant-based cooking classes or workshops can also enhance your skills and confidence in the kitchen. Many communities have plant-based restaurants and cafes where you can explore new dishes and gain inspiration for your own cooking.

Reading labels is essential when shopping for plant-based foods, especially if you are avoiding animal products entirely. Some packaged foods may contain hidden animal-derived ingredients like gelatin, casein, or whey. Familiarize yourself with common ingredients and look for certifications such as "vegan" or "plant-based" to guide your choices. Shopping at farmers' markets or local co-ops can provide access to fresh, seasonal produce and support local agriculture.

Adopting a plant-based diet is not just a personal health decision but a step towards a more sustainable and ethical lifestyle. By choosing more plant-based foods, you contribute to a reduction in environmental impact, promote animal welfare, and embrace a diet that aligns with principles of compassion and respect for all living beings. Whether you are motivated by health, environmental, or ethical reasons, a plant-based diet offers numerous benefits and opportunities for culinary exploration.

Protein Sources in Plant-Based Diets

Understanding where to get protein on a plant-based diet can initially seem challenging, given the widespread belief that meat, dairy, and eggs are the primary sources of this essential nutrient. However, a diverse range of plant-based foods can provide ample protein, ensuring that those who follow this diet can meet their nutritional needs without relying on animal products.

One of the most well-known and versatile sources of plant-based protein is legumes. This category includes beans, lentils, chickpeas, and peas, all of which are nutrient-dense and rich in protein. For example, a cup of cooked lentils delivers about 18 grams of protein, along with a hefty dose of fiber, iron, and folate. Black beans, kidney beans, and chickpeas offer similar benefits and can be used in various dishes like soups, stews, salads, and even baked goods. Peas, both fresh and dried, are another excellent source; split pea soup is a classic comfort food that packs a protein punch.

Tofu and tempeh, both made from soybeans, are staples in many plant-based diets. Tofu, also known as bean curd, is made by coagulating soy milk and pressing the curds into blocks. It comes in various textures, from silken to extra firm, making it suitable for a wide range of culinary applications. A half-cup serving of firm tofu contains about 10 grams of protein. Tempeh, on the other hand, is made from fermented whole soybeans, which gives it a nutty flavor and a firmer texture. It is even higher in protein than tofu, with a half-cup serving providing around 15 grams. Both tofu and tempeh absorb flavors well, making them ideal for marinades, stir-fries, and even grilling.

Edamame, or young soybeans, are another soy-based protein source. These bright green beans are often served as a snack or appetizer and can also be added to salads and grain bowls. A cup of edamame provides about 17 grams of protein, along with fiber, vitamins, and minerals. Their slightly sweet and nutty flavor makes them a popular choice for both children and adults.

Nuts and seeds are not only good sources of protein but also provide healthy fats, fiber, and a variety of vitamins and minerals. Almonds, walnuts, cashews, and pistachios can be eaten on their own as snacks, added to salads, or blended into nut butters. For example, a quarter-cup serving of almonds contains about 7 grams of protein. Similarly, seeds such as chia, flax, hemp, and sunflower seeds are protein-rich and can be sprinkled over breakfast cereals, yogurts, and salads. A tablespoon of chia seeds has about 2 grams of protein and is also a great source of omega-3 fatty acids.

Whole grains, while often overlooked as protein sources, can contribute significantly to daily protein intake. Quinoa, often referred to as a superfood, contains all nine essential amino acids, making it a complete protein. A cup of cooked quinoa provides 8 grams of protein. Other protein-rich grains include farro, barley, bulgur, and brown rice. These grains can be used as the base for bowls, in soups, or as side dishes to complement a variety of meals.

Vegetables, though not as protein-dense as legumes or soy products, can still contribute to protein intake, especially when consumed in large quantities. Broccoli, spinach, kale, Brussels sprouts, and artichokes are some examples of vegetables that contain notable amounts of protein. For instance, a cup of cooked spinach has about 5 grams of protein. Incorporating a variety of vegetables into your diet not only boosts protein intake but also ensures you receive a wide range of other essential nutrients.

Seitan, also known as wheat gluten, is another high-protein option for those on a plant-based diet. It has a meat-like texture, making it a popular choice for those transitioning from a meat-based diet. Seitan can be seasoned and cooked in numerous ways, providing a versatile protein source. A three-ounce serving of seitan contains an impressive 21 grams of protein. However, it's important to note that seitan is not suitable for those with gluten intolerance or celiac disease.

Plant-based protein powders can also be a convenient way to ensure adequate protein intake, especially for athletes or those with higher protein needs. These powders are made from various sources, including peas, brown rice, hemp, and pumpkin seeds. They can be easily added to smoothies, oatmeal, or baked goods. When choosing a protein powder, it's essential to look for one that is minimally processed and free from added sugars and artificial ingredients.

Incorporating a variety of these plant-based protein sources into your diet ensures that you receive all essential amino acids. While some plant foods are not complete proteins on their own, consuming a diverse range throughout the day can provide all the necessary amino acids your body needs. For example, pairing beans with rice or hummus with whole grain bread creates a complete protein.

Meal planning and preparation can be helpful strategies when transitioning to a plant-based diet. Taking the time to prepare protein-rich meals and snacks in advance ensures you have nutritious options readily available. Batch cooking beans, lentils, and grains, and storing them in the refrigerator or freezer, can save time and make it easier to assemble meals quickly. Preparing homemade snacks like trail mix with nuts and seeds or energy bars made from dates and nuts can also help maintain protein intake throughout the day.

Eating out or ordering in can sometimes pose challenges for those on a plant-based diet, but with a bit of planning, it's entirely manageable. Many restaurants now offer plant-based options, and it's always possible to modify dishes to include more protein. For example, you can ask for extra beans on a salad or substitute tofu for meat in a stir-fry. When traveling, packing protein-rich snacks like nuts, seeds, or protein bars can ensure you have nutritious options on hand.

Plant-Based Meal Planning

Navigating the world of plant-based meal planning can initially seem daunting, especially if you are accustomed to a diet heavy in meat and dairy. However, with a bit of organization and creativity, you can create nutritious, satisfying, and delicious meals that align with a plant-based lifestyle. The key lies in understanding the variety of plant-based foods available and learning how to combine them to ensure balanced nutrition.

A successful plant-based meal plan begins with understanding the foundational food groups: fruits, vegetables, grains, legumes, nuts, and seeds. Each of these groups provides unique nutrients essential for a balanced diet. Fruits and vegetables are rich in vitamins, minerals, and antioxidants. Grains, particularly whole grains, offer fiber and essential nutrients like B vitamins and iron. Legumes, including beans, lentils, and peas, are excellent protein sources and provide fiber and a range of vitamins and minerals. Nuts and seeds add healthy fats, protein, and various micronutrients.

Creating a weekly meal plan starts with selecting a variety of foods from each of these groups. Begin by planning your main meals—breakfast, lunch, and dinner—ensuring you include a balance of protein, carbohydrates, and fats in each. For breakfast, consider options like oatmeal topped with fresh fruits and nuts, a smoothie made with leafy greens, fruits, and a scoop of plant-based protein powder, or avocado toast on whole grain bread with a side of fruit. These meals are not only rich in nutrients but also quick and easy to prepare.

Lunch and dinner can be more varied, allowing for creativity and the inclusion of different cultural cuisines. Soups and stews are fantastic for incorporating a variety of vegetables and legumes. For example, a hearty lentil soup with carrots, celery, and spinach is both nourishing and filling. Salads are another versatile option; start with a base of leafy greens, then add a mix of colorful vegetables, a protein source like chickpeas or tofu, and a healthy fat such as avocado or a sprinkle of seeds. Grain bowls are also popular, combining cooked grains like quinoa or brown rice with roasted vegetables, a protein source, and a flavorful dressing or sauce.

Snacks are an essential part of meal planning, especially for maintaining energy levels throughout the day. Healthy, plant-based snacks can include fruit with a handful of nuts, hummus with vegetable sticks, or a small serving of whole grain crackers with nut butter. Preparing snacks in advance ensures you have nutritious options readily available, preventing the temptation to reach for less healthy alternatives.

One of the challenges in plant-based meal planning is ensuring you get enough protein. While it's a common concern, it's entirely possible to meet your protein needs through plant-based sources. Incorporate a variety of protein-rich foods like beans, lentils, tofu, tempeh, edamame, nuts, seeds, and whole grains into your meals. For instance, a serving of quinoa salad with black beans, corn, and a lime-tahini dressing provides a complete protein source, along with fiber and healthy fats.

Batch cooking and meal prepping can be game changers for maintaining a plant-based diet. Set aside a few hours each week to prepare large quantities of staple foods like grains, beans, and roasted vegetables. Store these components in the refrigerator or freezer, so you can easily assemble meals during the week. This approach not only saves time but also helps reduce food waste and ensures you always have healthy options on hand.

Variety is crucial in a plant-based diet to ensure you receive all essential nutrients. Rotate different types of grains, legumes, vegetables, fruits, nuts, and seeds to benefit from their unique nutrient profiles. For example, if you had quinoa and black beans one day, try brown rice and lentils the next. Experimenting with different cuisines can also introduce new flavors and foods into your diet, keeping meals exciting and diverse.

Spices and herbs are your best friends when it comes to adding flavor to plant-based meals. A well-stocked spice cabinet can transform simple ingredients into a gourmet feast. Curry powders, smoked paprika, cumin, turmeric, and fresh herbs like cilantro and basil can elevate the taste of your dishes. Don't be afraid to experiment with different combinations to find what you enjoy most.

Incorporating seasonal produce into your meal planning not only enhances the flavor and nutritional quality of your meals but can also be more cost-effective. Seasonal fruits and vegetables are often fresher and more affordable. Visit local farmers' markets or join a community-supported agriculture (CSA) program to get fresh, seasonal produce. This approach also supports local farmers and reduces the carbon footprint associated with transporting food long distances.

Staying hydrated is an often overlooked but crucial aspect of a plant-based diet. Water should be your primary beverage, but herbal teas, homemade fruit-infused waters, and occasional fresh juices can add variety. Limit sugary drinks and excessive caffeine, as they can lead to dehydration.

Eating out while following a plant-based diet can be enjoyable and manageable with a bit of planning. Many restaurants now offer plant-based options or are willing to make modifications upon request. When dining out, look for dishes that feature vegetables, grains, and legumes, and don't hesitate to ask for adjustments to make a meal plant-based. For example, you can request a vegetable stir-fry with tofu or a salad with extra beans and avocado.

Mindful eating is an important practice to incorporate into your meal planning. Take the time to enjoy your meals, savoring the flavors and textures of the food. This practice can improve digestion and enhance your overall eating experience. It also helps you tune into your body's hunger and fullness cues, promoting a healthier relationship with food.

To maintain motivation and inspiration, connect with the plant-based community. Join online forums, social media groups, or local meet-ups to share recipes, tips, and experiences. Engaging with others who share your dietary preferences can provide support and new ideas, making the plant-based journey more enjoyable.

Lastly, be patient and kind to yourself as you transition to a plant-based diet. It's a learning process, and it's okay to make mistakes or have occasional setbacks. Focus on progress rather than perfection, and celebrate the positive changes you're making for your health and the environment.

Delicious and Nutritious Plant-Based Recipes

Imagine the aroma of a sizzling stir-fry wafting through your kitchen, the vibrant colors of fresh vegetables mingling in a pan, the promise of a meal that is both delicious and nourishing. Transitioning to a plant-based diet does not mean sacrificing flavor or satisfaction. In fact, the world of plant-based cuisine offers an abundance of delicious and nutritious recipes that can delight your taste buds and invigorate your health. Let's dive into a selection of these recipes, each crafted to bring joy and vitality to your dining experience.

First, let's start with a breakfast that's both hearty and energizing: the classic smoothie bowl. Begin by blending a frozen banana with a cup of spinach, half a cup of frozen berries, and a splash of almond milk until smooth. Pour the thick, creamy blend into a bowl and top with granola, sliced kiwi, chia seeds, and a drizzle of almond butter. This vibrant bowl is not only visually appealing but packed with vitamins, antioxidants, and fiber, providing a nutritious start to your day.

For a mid-morning snack, consider baked sweet potato fries. Preheat your oven to 425°F (220°C). Slice a large sweet potato into thin strips, toss with olive oil, paprika, garlic powder, and a pinch of salt, then spread them out on a baking sheet. Bake for 25-30 minutes, flipping halfway through, until they are crispy and golden. Sweet potatoes are a fantastic source of beta-carotene, fiber, and complex carbohydrates, making this snack both satisfying and beneficial for sustained energy.

Lunchtime offers an opportunity to get creative with a quinoa and black bean salad. Cook one cup of quinoa according to the package instructions and let it cool. In a large bowl, combine the cooked quinoa with a can of rinsed black beans, a cup of corn, diced red bell pepper, chopped cilantro, and sliced cherry tomatoes. For the dressing, whisk together the juice of two limes, a tablespoon of olive oil, a teaspoon of cumin, and a pinch of salt and pepper. Toss the salad with the dressing and serve chilled. This dish is a powerhouse of protein, fiber, and essential nutrients, perfect for a midday meal.

For an afternoon pick-me-up, try a handful of spiced nuts. In a skillet over medium heat, toast a cup of mixed nuts until fragrant. Add a tablespoon of maple syrup, a teaspoon of smoked paprika, and a pinch of sea salt, stirring to coat the nuts evenly. Let them cool before enjoying. Nuts are rich in healthy fats, protein, and various vitamins and minerals, providing a nutritious and energizing snack.

Dinner can be a comforting and flavorful experience with a bowl of lentil and vegetable curry. Start by heating a tablespoon of coconut oil in a large pot. Sauté a diced onion, two minced garlic cloves, and a tablespoon of grated ginger until fragrant. Add a cup of red lentils, a can of diced tomatoes, and three cups of vegetable broth. Stir in a teaspoon each of turmeric, cumin, and coriander, and simmer for 20 minutes. Add chopped vegetables such as carrots, zucchini, and spinach, and cook for another 10 minutes until the lentils and vegetables are tender. Serve the curry over steamed brown rice, garnished with fresh cilantro. This dish is rich in protein, fiber, and a variety of vitamins and minerals, making it both nourishing and satisfying.

For dessert, indulge in a serving of chocolate avocado mousse. Blend two ripe avocados with a quarter cup of cocoa powder, a quarter cup of maple syrup, a teaspoon of vanilla extract, and a pinch of salt until smooth and creamy. Chill the mousse for an hour before serving, topped with fresh berries or a sprinkle of cacao nibs. This dessert is decadent yet nutritious, providing healthy fats, antioxidants, and a delightful chocolate flavor.

Let's not forget the importance of staying hydrated and enjoying refreshing beverages. A simple yet delightful option is a cucumber-mint infused water. Slice half a cucumber and add it to a pitcher of water along with a handful of fresh mint leaves. Let it steep in the refrigerator for a few hours before serving. This refreshing drink not only helps with hydration but also adds a subtle flavor that makes drinking water more enjoyable.

Another fantastic recipe for breakfast is a savory tofu scramble. Crumble a block of firm tofu into a skillet with a tablespoon of olive oil over medium heat. Add a teaspoon of turmeric, a teaspoon of nutritional yeast, and a pinch of salt and pepper. Sauté the tofu until it's heated through and slightly crispy, then mix in chopped vegetables such as bell peppers, spinach, and cherry tomatoes. Serve the scramble with whole grain toast or wrapped in a tortilla for a delicious and protein-packed breakfast.

If you're seeking a light yet fulfilling lunch, consider a Mediterranean chickpea salad. In a large bowl, combine a can of rinsed chickpeas, a cup of diced cucumber, halved cherry tomatoes, sliced red onion, and chopped parsley. For the dressing, whisk together the juice of one lemon, a tablespoon of olive oil, a teaspoon of dried oregano, and a pinch of salt and pepper. Toss the salad with the dressing and serve. This salad is a perfect blend of flavors and textures, providing protein, fiber, and a range of essential nutrients.

For an afternoon treat, a slice of banana bread can be both comforting and nutritious. Preheat your oven to 350°F (175°C). In a large bowl, mash three ripe bananas and mix with a quarter cup of melted coconut oil, half a cup of maple syrup, and a teaspoon of vanilla extract. In a separate bowl, combine one and a half cups of whole wheat flour, a teaspoon of baking soda, and a pinch of salt. Gradually add the dry ingredients to the wet mixture, stirring until just combined. Pour the batter into a greased loaf pan and bake for 50-60 minutes, or until a toothpick inserted into the center comes out clean. This banana bread is moist, flavorful, and packed with natural sweetness and fiber.

Dinner can be elevated with a roasted vegetable and hummus wrap. Spread a generous amount of hummus on a whole grain tortilla. Layer with roasted vegetables such as bell peppers, zucchini, and eggplant, which you can prepare by tossing them in olive oil, salt, and pepper, and roasting at 400°F (200°C) for 20-25 minutes. Add fresh greens like arugula or spinach, and roll up the tortilla. This wrap is a delightful combination of creamy, crunchy, and savory elements, making it a satisfying and nutritious meal.

To finish the day on a sweet note, enjoy a bowl of chia pudding. In a jar, combine three tablespoons of chia seeds with a cup of almond milk, a tablespoon of maple syrup, and a teaspoon of vanilla extract. Stir well and let it sit in the refrigerator for at least four hours, or overnight, to thicken. Before serving, give it a good stir and top with fresh fruit, nuts, or a drizzle of almond butter. This dessert is rich in omega-3 fatty acids, fiber, and a host of other nutrients, making it a healthy and delicious way to end your day.

Tips for Transitioning to a Plant-Based Diet

Embarking on a journey toward a plant-based diet can be both exciting and daunting. Whether you're motivated by health, environmental concerns, or ethical reasons, making the shift requires thoughtful planning and a willingness to embrace new foods and habits. Here are some practical tips to help you transition smoothly and enjoyably to a plant-based lifestyle.

Start by gradually incorporating more plant-based meals into your daily routine. Rather than overhauling your entire diet overnight, begin with a few meatless days each week. This approach allows your palate to adjust and gives you time to explore and learn about plant-based options. For instance, you might replace your usual breakfast with a hearty bowl of oatmeal topped with fruits and nuts or swap out your typical lunch sandwich for a vibrant quinoa salad packed with vegetables and beans.

One of the most effective strategies for a successful transition is to focus on what you can add to your diet rather than what you need to eliminate. Explore the vast array of fruits, vegetables, grains, legumes, nuts, and seeds available to you. Experiment with new recipes and cooking techniques to keep your meals interesting and satisfying. For example, try roasting chickpeas for a crunchy snack, or make a creamy cashew-based sauce to drizzle over roasted vegetables.

Stocking your pantry with essential plant-based staples is crucial. Items such as lentils, beans, quinoa, brown rice, oats, chia seeds, and a variety of nuts and seeds can form the foundation of many nutritious meals. Having these ingredients on hand makes it easier to prepare quick and healthy dishes. Additionally, keep a selection of your favorite spices and herbs to enhance the flavors of your meals. Spices like cumin, turmeric, paprika, and herbs like basil, cilantro, and parsley can transform simple ingredients into delicious, aromatic dishes.

Meal planning and preparation can make the transition smoother and help you stay on track. Set aside some time each week to plan your meals, make a shopping list, and prep ingredients. Cooking in batches can save you time and ensure you have ready-to-eat meals throughout the week. For example, you might cook a big pot of vegetable stew or lentil soup that you can enjoy for several meals. Preparing overnight oats or chia pudding the night before can also provide you with quick and nutritious breakfast options.

Eating out and socializing can present challenges when transitioning to a plant-based diet, but they are far from insurmountable. When dining out, research restaurants in advance to find those that offer plant-based options. Many restaurants now cater to various dietary preferences and are happy to accommodate vegan requests. Don't hesitate to ask the server about modifying dishes to make them plant-based. For example, you might request a vegetable stir-fry without the meat or cheese, or ask for a salad with extra beans and avocado instead of chicken.

Social gatherings can also be navigated successfully with a bit of preparation. If you're attending a potluck or dinner party, consider bringing a plant-based dish to share. This ensures you have something to eat and introduces others to delicious plant-based cuisine. Communicating your dietary choices to friends and family in advance can help them accommodate your needs and avoid any awkward situations.

Understanding your nutritional needs is essential when transitioning to a plant-based diet. While a well-planned plant-based diet can provide all the necessary nutrients, certain vitamins and minerals require attention. For instance, vitamin B12, which is primarily found in animal products, should be supplemented or obtained from fortified foods. Ensure you get enough iron by consuming iron-rich foods like lentils, chickpeas, tofu, quinoa, and dark leafy greens, and pair them with vitamin C-rich foods to enhance absorption. Omega-3 fatty acids, important for heart and brain health, can be sourced from flaxseeds, chia seeds, walnuts, and algae-based supplements.

Protein is another nutrient that often concerns those new to a plant-based diet, but there are plenty of plant-based protein sources available. Legumes, tofu, tempeh, edamame, seitan, quinoa, and a variety of nuts and seeds provide ample protein to meet your needs. Incorporating a mix of these foods throughout your meals ensures you get a balanced intake of essential amino acids.

Listening to your body and making adjustments as needed is important. Everyone's nutritional needs and responses to dietary changes are different. Pay attention to how you feel and consult with a healthcare professional or a registered dietitian if you have specific concerns or questions. They can provide personalized guidance and help you create a balanced and satisfying plant-based diet.

Staying informed and inspired is crucial for maintaining motivation and enthusiasm. There are numerous resources available, from cookbooks and blogs to documentaries and social media communities, that can provide recipes, tips, and support. Engaging with others who share your dietary goals can offer a sense of community and encouragement. Joining local or online groups focused on plant-based living can connect you with like-minded individuals and provide a platform for sharing experiences and advice.

As you transition, be kind to yourself and remember that perfection is not the goal. It's normal to encounter challenges and occasional slip-ups. What's important is your overall progress and commitment to making positive changes. Celebrate your successes, no matter how small, and use any setbacks as learning opportunities.

Exploring seasonal and local produce can enhance your plant-based journey. Visiting farmers' markets or joining a community-supported agriculture (CSA) program can introduce you to fresh, locally-grown fruits and vegetables. Seasonal produce is often more flavorful and nutrient-dense, and supporting local farmers contributes to a more sustainable food system. Experimenting with seasonal ingredients can inspire creativity in the kitchen and add variety to your meals.

Another practical tip is to familiarize yourself with plant-based substitutes for common animal products. For example, nutritional yeast can provide a cheesy flavor to dishes without dairy, and flax or chia seeds mixed with water can serve as an egg substitute in baking. Plant-based milks, such as almond, soy, or oat milk, can replace cow's milk in most recipes. These substitutes can make the transition easier by allowing you to continue enjoying your favorite dishes in a plant-based form.

Incorporating mindfulness into your eating habits can also support your transition. Mindful eating involves paying attention to the sensory experience of eating, including the taste, texture, and aroma of food, as well as recognizing hunger and fullness cues. This practice can enhance your appreciation of plant-based foods and help you make more intentional and satisfying food choices.

Lastly, don't underestimate the power of variety and balance in your diet. Eating a diverse range of foods ensures you get a wide spectrum of nutrients and prevents dietary monotony. Aim to include a colorful assortment of fruits and vegetables, different types of grains, and a variety of protein sources in your meals. Experimenting with global cuisines can also add excitement and diversity to your diet. Many cultures have rich traditions of plant-based dishes, such as Indian curries, Middle Eastern falafel, and Mexican bean-based dishes.

Chapter 5

Reducing Food Waste

Understanding Food Waste and Its Impact

Food waste is an issue of staggering proportions, affecting every corner of the globe. Each year, roughly one-third of all food produced for human consumption is wasted—amounting to about 1.3 billion tons. This waste occurs at various stages of the food supply chain: during production, post-harvest processing, distribution, retail, and ultimately within households. Understanding the multifaceted impact of food waste is crucial for developing strategies to mitigate it and promote a more sustainable world.

At the production level, food waste can result from inefficient harvesting practices, pests, and diseases, as well as adverse weather conditions. For instance, crops may be left unharvested due to market price fluctuations, making it economically unviable for farmers to collect them. Post-harvest losses often occur due to inadequate storage facilities, leading to spoilage from pests, fungi, or improper temperature control. In developing countries, these challenges are particularly acute due to limited access to modern agricultural technologies and infrastructure.

Once food reaches the distribution phase, waste can occur during transportation and handling. Perishable items such as fruits, vegetables, dairy, and meat are especially vulnerable to spoilage if not handled properly. Poor packaging, delays in transport, and lack of refrigeration can all contribute to significant losses. In retail environments, food waste often stems from overstocking, improper stock rotation, and stringent aesthetic standards that lead to the discarding of perfectly edible food simply because it doesn't meet visual criteria.

Consumers play a significant role in the food waste equation as well. In households, food waste can result from over-purchasing, improper storage, lack of meal planning, and confusion over food labeling. Many people misinterpret "best before" and "use by" dates, discarding food that is still safe to eat. Additionally, impulse buying and buying in bulk, driven by attractive sales and promotions, often lead to more food than can be consumed before it spoils.

The environmental impact of food waste is profound. When food is wasted, so too are the resources used to produce it, including water, land, energy, labor, and capital. Agriculture is a major user of water resources; for example, it takes about 1,800 gallons of water to produce a pound of beef and around 120 gallons for a pound of potatoes. Therefore, when food is discarded, the water footprint of that food is also wasted. Furthermore, food waste contributes significantly to greenhouse gas emissions. When organic waste decomposes anaerobically in landfills, it produces methane, a potent greenhouse gas with a global warming potential many times that of carbon dioxide.

Economically, food waste represents a massive loss. The financial cost of food waste is estimated to be in the hundreds of billions of dollars annually. For businesses, reducing food waste can directly improve the bottom line by lowering disposal costs and increasing operational efficiency. For consumers, minimizing food waste can result in significant savings on grocery bills.

Addressing food waste requires a multifaceted approach involving various stakeholders, including governments, businesses, and individuals. Policy interventions can play a crucial role in reducing food waste. Governments can implement regulations to standardize food labeling, making it clearer and more consistent to help consumers make better decisions about food safety and shelf life. Additionally, policies that incentivize food donation and redistribution can help ensure that surplus food reaches those in need rather than ending up in landfills.

Businesses, particularly those in the food industry, have a critical role to play. Retailers can adopt better inventory management practices and use technology to track and predict demand more accurately. Reducing portion sizes and offering flexible portion options in restaurants can help minimize plate waste. Food manufacturers and retailers can also collaborate with food banks and charities to redistribute surplus food. Moreover, innovations in packaging that extend shelf life and improve the ability to monitor freshness can also contribute to reducing waste.

At the consumer level, raising awareness about the impact of food waste and promoting behavioral changes are essential. Simple practices such as planning meals, creating shopping lists, storing food properly, and understanding food labels can significantly reduce household food waste. Educational campaigns can highlight the environmental and economic costs of food waste, encouraging more mindful consumption habits.

Community initiatives can also be effective in tackling food waste. Programs that facilitate the sharing of surplus food within communities, such as community fridges and food-sharing apps, can help redistribute excess food. Composting programs can turn food scraps into valuable compost for gardening and agriculture, reducing the amount of organic waste sent to landfills.

Technological advancements offer promising solutions to the food waste problem. Apps that connect consumers with surplus food from restaurants and retailers at reduced prices can help divert food that would otherwise be discarded. Smart kitchen devices that monitor food inventory and suggest recipes based on what's available can help households use up ingredients before they spoil. Additionally, advancements in agricultural technology, such as precision farming and improved storage techniques, can reduce losses at the production and post-harvest stages.

The fight against food waste is also a social justice issue. While millions of tons of food are wasted, millions of people around the world go hungry. Ensuring that surplus food reaches those in need can help address food insecurity and promote a more equitable food system. Organizations that rescue food and distribute it to those in need play a vital role in this effort. Supporting these organizations through donations, volunteering, and advocacy can amplify their impact.

On a global scale, international cooperation is vital to addressing food waste. Sharing best practices, research, and technological innovations across borders can help countries develop effective strategies tailored to their specific contexts. Collaborative efforts can also address systemic issues in global supply chains that contribute to food waste.

Ultimately, reducing food waste requires a shift in how we value food. Recognizing the resources and effort that go into producing the food we eat can foster a greater appreciation and a more mindful approach to consumption. By making conscious choices, advocating for policy changes, and supporting community initiatives, we can all contribute to a more sustainable and equitable food system.

How to Shop Smart and Reduce Waste

Navigating the aisles of a grocery store can be overwhelming, leading to impulse buys and often, unfortunately, to waste. Shopping smartly isn't just about saving money; it's also about making conscious choices that contribute to a more sustainable lifestyle. By adopting a few strategic habits, you can significantly reduce food waste, stretching your budget further and minimizing your environmental footprint.

The first step to shopping smart is meticulous planning. Before heading to the store, take inventory of your pantry, refrigerator, and freezer. Knowing what you already have prevents duplicate purchases and helps in meal planning. Create a meal plan for the week, considering breakfasts, lunches, dinners, and snacks. Include a variety of meals that use similar ingredients to ensure nothing goes to waste. For example, if you buy a bunch of cilantro for a recipe, plan another dish that uses the rest of it before it goes bad.

Once you have your meal plan, draft a detailed shopping list. Lists are crucial; they keep you focused on what you need and help you avoid unnecessary items. Break down your list by categories such as produce, dairy, grains, and proteins, mirroring the layout of the store to streamline your shopping trip. Stick to the list as much as possible, but allow some flexibility for unplanned discounts on items you frequently use.

Timing your shopping trip is another smart strategy. Try to shop when the store is less crowded, allowing you to make thoughtful decisions without rushing. Additionally, avoid shopping on an empty stomach. Hunger can lead to impulse buys and unhealthy choices, often resulting in more perishable items than you can consume.

Pay attention to portion sizes and packaging. Bulk buying can be economical and reduce packaging waste, but only if you can properly store and consume the quantities purchased. For items with a longer shelf life like grains, pasta, and canned goods, buying in bulk makes sense. For perishables like fruits, vegetables, and dairy, smaller, more frequent purchases may be better to avoid spoilage.

Understanding food labels is crucial. "Best before" dates indicate quality, not safety. Foods may still be safe to eat past this date but might not be at their peak flavor or texture. "Use by" dates are more critical, especially for perishable items, as they indicate the last date recommended for safe consumption. Being aware of these distinctions can help you prioritize the use of items in your kitchen and reduce wastage.

While shopping, select fresh produce carefully. Choose items that are not overly ripe unless you plan to use them immediately. Slightly underripe fruits and vegetables will last longer and give you more flexibility in your meal planning. For example, green bananas can ripen at home, giving you a few extra days to enjoy them.

Consider the packaging of the products you buy. Opt for loose, unpackaged produce when possible to reduce plastic waste. Bring your own reusable bags for produce and bulk items. Some stores allow customers to bring their own containers for deli and bulk foods, further cutting down on single-use plastics.

Frozen and canned foods are excellent alternatives to fresh produce, especially for items that are out of season or have a short shelf life. Frozen fruits and vegetables are often picked and frozen at peak ripeness, retaining their nutritional value and flavor. Canned goods, such as beans, tomatoes, and fish, are long-lasting pantry staples that can reduce the need for frequent shopping trips.

When it comes to proteins, consider the shelf life and storage options. Fresh meat, poultry, and fish should be consumed within a few days of purchase or frozen for later use. Buying smaller quantities more frequently ensures freshness and prevents waste. Plant-based proteins, such as beans, lentils, and tofu, often have longer shelf lives and can be stored in the pantry or refrigerator.

Dairy products can be a significant source of food waste due to their perishability. Opt for smaller containers if you don't consume dairy frequently. Shelf-stable alternatives, like powdered milk or plant-based milks, can be useful backups. Cheese can be bought in blocks and shredded or sliced at home, reducing packaging waste and allowing you to use only what you need.

Bread and baked goods are another common source of waste. Store bread in the freezer if you don't plan to use it within a few days. Slices can be toasted directly from frozen, ensuring you always have fresh bread on hand. Consider buying whole loaves from a bakery where you can request specific quantities, reducing the risk of overbuying.

Impulse buying can sabotage even the best-laid plans. Stores are designed to encourage extra purchases with strategic product placement and enticing displays. Stay focused on your list, but allow for occasional treats in moderation. Be mindful of special offers and bulk deals; they are only cost-effective if you will use the items before they expire.

Shopping locally and seasonally can also help reduce waste. Local produce is often fresher and has a longer shelf life because it doesn't spend as much time in transit. Seasonal items are typically abundant and less expensive, making them a smart choice for both your wallet and the environment. Farmers' markets and local food co-ops are excellent places to find fresh, seasonal produce.

Mindful storage at home is the final step to reducing food waste. Store perishables like fruits and vegetables in the appropriate areas of your refrigerator. Leafy greens and herbs last longer when stored in damp paper towels or in breathable produce bags. Keep your refrigerator organized, with older items at the front, so they are used first. Label leftovers with dates and prioritize their use in your meal planning.

Recipes that utilize leftovers creatively can further minimize waste. Soups, stews, and casseroles are perfect for using up vegetables nearing the end of their shelf life. Fruit that is past its prime can be used in smoothies, baked goods, or jams. Bread that has gone stale can be turned into croutons, bread pudding, or breadcrumbs.

Creative Uses for Leftovers

Leftovers often get a bad rap. They are frequently relegated to the back of the fridge, only to be forgotten and eventually thrown away. Yet, with a bit of creativity and resourcefulness, leftovers can become the star of your next meal. Transforming yesterday's dinner into today's culinary delight not only reduces food waste but also saves time and money. Embracing leftovers as an opportunity for creativity can lead to delicious discoveries and a more sustainable kitchen.

One of the simplest ways to breathe new life into leftovers is through soups and stews. Almost any leftover meat or vegetable can find a second life in a hearty soup. Start with a base of onions, garlic, and perhaps some celery or carrots, then add in your leftover proteins or vegetables. A chicken breast from last night's dinner can be shredded and added to a pot with some broth, a can of beans, and whatever vegetables you have on hand. Season with herbs and spices, and let it simmer until the flavors meld together. The result is a comforting and nutritious meal that hardly feels like a repeat.

Leftover grains and pasta also lend themselves well to creative repurposing. Cooked rice, quinoa, or couscous can be transformed into a refreshing salad. Simply mix the grains with chopped vegetables, a protein source like beans or leftover chicken, and a zesty dressing. This makes for a quick and satisfying lunch. Similarly, leftover pasta can become a pasta salad with the addition of some fresh vegetables, cheese, and a tangy vinaigrette. Alternatively, toss the pasta with some olive oil, garlic, and whatever vegetables or meat you have, and bake it with a sprinkling of cheese for a comforting casserole.

Another versatile use for leftovers is in stir-fries. Almost any combination of vegetables and proteins can be quickly sautéed with some garlic, ginger, and soy sauce for a fast and flavorful meal. Leftover rice can be turned into fried rice by cooking it with some vegetables, an egg, and a splash of soy sauce. The key to a good stir-fry or fried rice is to have all your ingredients prepped and ready to go before you start cooking, as the process moves quickly.

Leftover roasted or grilled meats can be particularly versatile. Slice them thinly and use them in sandwiches or wraps for an easy lunch option. They can also be added to salads, grain bowls, or even used as a topping for homemade pizzas. If you have leftover steak, thinly slice it and serve it over a bed of greens with some blue cheese and a balsamic vinaigrette for a hearty salad. Leftover chicken can be shredded and used in tacos, enchiladas, or quesadillas.

Vegetables are often the most challenging leftovers to use creatively, but they offer plenty of possibilities. Roasted vegetables can be pureed with some broth and cream to make a silky soup. They can also be added to omelets, frittatas, or quiches for a quick and nutritious breakfast or brunch. Another option is to mix leftover vegetables into a grain salad or toss them with some pasta and olive oil for a simple yet satisfying meal.

Bread is another commonly wasted food that can be repurposed in many delicious ways. Stale bread can be turned into croutons by cutting it into cubes, tossing it with some olive oil and seasoning, and baking it until crispy. These croutons can then be used to add crunch to salads or soups. Another option is to make bread pudding, a comforting dessert that transforms stale bread into a rich and custardy treat. Simply soak the bread in a mixture of eggs, milk, sugar, and vanilla, then bake until set.

For those with a sweet tooth, leftover fruits can be used in a variety of desserts. Overripe bananas are perfect for banana bread or muffins. Apples that are starting to soften can be cooked down with some sugar and cinnamon to make a delicious applesauce or filling for a pie. Berries that are past their prime can be blended into smoothies or cooked with a bit of sugar to make a quick jam or sauce for pancakes.

Embracing a zero-waste kitchen doesn't mean sacrificing flavor or variety. In fact, using leftovers creatively often leads to discovering new favorite dishes. It encourages flexibility and innovation, allowing you to adapt recipes based on what you have rather than what you need to buy. This not only reduces waste but also fosters a deeper appreciation for the food you have and the meals you create.

Moreover, incorporating leftovers into your cooking routine can save significant time and effort. Cooking once and eating twice (or more) means less time spent in the kitchen and more time enjoying your meals. It also means fewer trips to the grocery store, which saves both time and money.

To make the most of your leftovers, proper storage is essential. Store leftovers in clear, airtight containers so you can easily see what you have. Label containers with the date to keep track of how long items have been in the fridge. Most leftovers are best used within three to four days, but some items, like soups and casseroles, can be frozen for longer storage. When reheating leftovers, make sure they are heated thoroughly to ensure they are safe to eat.

Involving the whole family in the process of repurposing leftovers can also be a fun and educational experience. Encourage kids to come up with creative ways to use what's in the fridge. This not only teaches them important cooking skills but also instills a value for reducing waste and thinking resourcefully.

Ultimately, the key to making the most of leftovers is to view them not as scraps but as opportunities. With a bit of imagination, yesterday's dinner can become today's lunch or even tomorrow's breakfast. Each meal becomes a stepping stone to the next, creating a continuous cycle of creativity and sustainability in your kitchen.

Composting at Home

Composting at home is a simple yet profoundly impactful way to reduce waste and enrich your garden. It transforms organic waste into valuable nutrients for your plants, reducing the amount of garbage sent to landfills and enhancing soil health. While the process might seem daunting at first, it can be easily managed with a bit of knowledge and some basic tools. Let's delve into the practical steps and benefits of home composting, ensuring you can turn your kitchen scraps and yard waste into "black gold" for your garden.

Begin your composting journey by selecting an appropriate composting system. Various options cater to different needs and spaces, including compost bins, tumblers, and open piles. For those with limited space, a compost tumbler or a small bin can fit neatly on a balcony or in a small backyard. Larger yards can accommodate open piles or larger bins, which can process more waste. Whichever system you choose, ensure it has good air circulation and is easy to access for adding materials and turning the compost.

Once you have your composting system in place, start by gathering your compostable materials. Composting relies on a balance of "green" and "brown" materials. Green materials are rich in nitrogen and include kitchen scraps like fruit and vegetable peels, coffee grounds, and fresh grass clippings. Brown materials, which provide carbon, include dried leaves, straw, cardboard, and paper. Aim for a roughly equal mix of green and brown materials to maintain a healthy compost pile.

As you add materials to your compost, chop or shred larger pieces to speed up the decomposition process. Smaller pieces break down more quickly, allowing the microbes responsible for composting to work more efficiently. For instance, cutting up apple cores or tearing cardboard into smaller chunks can make a significant difference in how fast your compost matures.

Layering is another crucial aspect of effective composting. Start with a layer of coarse materials like straw or small branches to promote air circulation at the bottom of your compost pile or bin. Alternate layers of green and brown materials, ensuring that each layer is moist but not waterlogged. Moisture is essential for the decomposition process, but too much water can create anaerobic conditions, leading to unpleasant odors and slower composting.

Turning your compost pile regularly is vital for aerating the material and speeding up decomposition. Use a garden fork or compost aerator to mix the pile every few weeks, ensuring that oxygen reaches the center of the pile. This process helps maintain the aerobic conditions necessary for efficient composting and prevents the pile from becoming compacted. A well-turned compost pile will break down much faster and more evenly.

Monitoring the temperature of your compost pile can also provide insights into its progress. A healthy compost pile generates heat as microbes break down the organic material. The ideal temperature range for composting is between 120°F and 160°F. If your compost pile feels cool to the touch, it might need more green materials or more frequent turning to boost microbial activity. Conversely, if it's too hot, adding more brown materials and turning the pile can help regulate the temperature.

Pest management is another consideration when composting at home. To avoid attracting rodents and other pests, avoid adding meat, dairy products, and oily foods to your compost. These items can create strong odors that attract unwanted visitors. Instead, focus on plant-based kitchen scraps and yard waste. If you notice pests around your compost bin, ensure it is securely closed and consider using a bin with a pest-proof design.

Composting can be a year-round activity, even in colder climates. While decomposition slows down during the winter months, it doesn't stop entirely. Insulating your compost pile with straw or a tarp can help retain heat and keep the composting process going. Additionally, continue adding materials throughout the winter, as the pile will resume active decomposition when temperatures rise in the spring.

The end product of composting, known as humus, is a rich, dark substance teeming with nutrients and beneficial microbes. It can significantly improve soil structure, water retention, and fertility. When your compost is ready, it should be dark and crumbly with an earthy smell. To use your finished compost, spread it over your garden beds, mix it into the soil, or use it as a top dressing for potted plants. The nutrients in the compost will gradually release, providing a steady supply of nourishment for your plants.

Vermicomposting is another excellent composting method for those with limited space or a desire for an indoor composting option. This method uses worms, typically red wigglers, to break down food scraps quickly and efficiently. A vermicomposting bin can be kept indoors, providing a convenient way to compost kitchen waste year-round. The resulting worm castings are an exceptionally nutrient-rich form of compost, perfect for boosting plant growth.

Starting a composting routine can also foster a deeper connection to the natural cycles of growth and decay. It encourages mindfulness about the waste we produce and the potential to repurpose it into something beneficial. Composting can become a family activity, teaching children about sustainability and the importance of recycling organic materials.

Additionally, composting at home contributes to broader environmental benefits. Organic waste in landfills decomposes anaerobically, producing methane, a potent greenhouse gas. By composting at home, you help reduce methane emissions and contribute to a healthier planet. Moreover, composting reduces the need for chemical fertilizers, which can have harmful environmental impacts. The natural nutrients in compost support plant health without the risk of chemical runoff into waterways.

For those interested in taking their composting efforts even further, consider community composting programs. These initiatives allow neighborhoods to collectively compost organic waste, often using larger-scale systems that can handle more material. Participating in a community composting program can enhance your composting capabilities and foster a sense of community around sustainable practices.

Zero-Waste Recipes

Cooking with a zero-waste mindset can transform your kitchen into a hub of sustainability and creativity. By utilizing every part of the ingredients you buy, you not only reduce your environmental impact but also maximize the nutritional value and flavor of your meals. Zero-waste recipes are about making the most of what you have, minimizing waste, and discovering delicious and innovative ways to use food that might otherwise be discarded.

One of the key principles of zero-waste cooking is to plan your meals around what you already have on hand. Before heading to the grocery store, take stock of your pantry, fridge, and freezer. This helps avoid purchasing unnecessary items and ensures you use up ingredients before they spoil. For instance, if you have a surplus of vegetables nearing their prime, plan a hearty vegetable soup or a stir-fry to make the most of them.

Another essential aspect of zero-waste recipes is incorporating every part of the ingredient. For example, when preparing vegetables, don't throw away the peels, stems, or leaves. Carrot tops can be blended into a vibrant pesto, potato peels can be baked into crispy snacks, and broccoli stems can be sliced thinly and added to stir-fries or salads. These parts often contain valuable nutrients and flavors that are too good to waste.

One popular zero-waste recipe is vegetable broth made from kitchen scraps. Save the ends, peels, and trimmings of vegetables like onions, carrots, celery, and garlic in a container in your freezer. Once you have a sufficient amount, simmer the scraps in water with some herbs and spices for a few hours, then strain to create a flavorful broth. This homemade broth can be used as a base for soups, stews, and risottos, adding depth and richness to your dishes.

Leftovers are another critical component of zero-waste cooking. Instead of seeing them as remnants of previous meals, view them as opportunities for new creations. Leftover rice can be transformed into fried rice or rice pudding. Stale bread can become croutons, breadcrumbs, or a savory bread pudding. Even small amounts of leftover meat or vegetables can be incorporated into omelets, quesadillas, or pasta dishes.

Consider embracing the art of pickling and fermenting to extend the life of your produce. Cucumbers, radishes, carrots, and even watermelon rinds can be pickled to create tangy, crunchy snacks that last much longer than their fresh counterparts. Fermenting cabbage into sauerkraut or making kimchi not only preserves vegetables but also enhances their nutritional value with beneficial probiotics.

Zero-waste recipes also encourage the use of bulk bins and reusable containers to minimize packaging waste. Purchasing grains, nuts, seeds, and spices in bulk allows you to buy only the amount you need, reducing excess and packaging waste. Bring your own containers to the store to eliminate single-use plastic bags and contribute to a more sustainable shopping experience.

Eggshells, often discarded without a second thought, can be repurposed in surprising ways. Rinse and dry them, then grind into a fine powder to use as a calcium supplement for your garden or even in homemade toothpaste. The egg cartons themselves can be composted or used to start seedlings for your garden.

Herbs are another ingredient where zero-waste principles can shine. When you buy a bunch of herbs, it's common to use a few sprigs and let the rest wilt. Instead, freeze leftover herbs in olive oil using an ice cube tray, creating ready-to-use portions for future cooking. Herb stems, often discarded, can add flavor to stocks or be blended into sauces.

Animal products can also be utilized more fully in a zero-waste kitchen. For instance, bones from roasted chicken or beef can be simmered to make a nutrient-rich bone broth. This broth can be used as a base for soups or stews, providing a rich source of collagen and minerals. Even fat trimmings can be rendered down into cooking fat, reducing the need to purchase additional oils.

One of the more creative aspects of zero-waste cooking involves dessert. Overripe fruits, which might otherwise be thrown out, can be transformed into jams, compotes, or baked goods. Bananas that are too soft for eating can become banana bread or pancakes. Apples with bruises can be cooked down into applesauce or used in pies and crisps.

Beverages are another area where zero-waste principles can apply. Used coffee grounds and tea leaves can be composted or used in the garden as fertilizer. Citrus peels can be dried and used to infuse water or spirits, or even transformed into candied treats. Leftover wine can be turned into vinegar, and vegetable scraps can be used to brew homemade vegetable stock.

Cooking with a zero-waste mindset also means being flexible and creative with your recipes. Don't be afraid to substitute ingredients based on what you have on hand. If a recipe calls for spinach but you have kale, go ahead and swap them. If you're missing a specific herb, try using another one that's available. This adaptability not only reduces waste but also encourages you to experiment and discover new flavor combinations.

Involving the whole family in zero-waste cooking can be both educational and fun. Children can learn about the importance of reducing waste and how to be creative in the kitchen. Encourage them to help with tasks like saving vegetable scraps, making stock, or creating new dishes from leftovers. This involvement fosters a sense of responsibility and creativity, making the kitchen a place of learning and experimentation.

Zero-waste cooking extends beyond the kitchen itself. It encourages a holistic approach to food, from mindful shopping and meal planning to creative use of leftovers and scraps. By adopting these practices, you contribute to a more sustainable food system and reduce your environmental footprint.

Incorporating zero-waste recipes into your routine doesn't have to be overwhelming. Start small by gradually introducing these practices and building a habit of mindful cooking. Over time, these efforts will become second nature, leading to a more sustainable and efficient kitchen.

www.ingramcontent.com/pod-product-compliance
Lightning Source LLC
Chambersburg PA
CBHW050543160726
48003CB00002B/729